ELIZABETH ZIMMERMANN'S

KNITTER'S ALMANAC

Projects for Each Month of the Year

Photographs by Tom Zimmermann
Drawings by the Author

DOVER PUBLICATIONS, INC., NEW YORK

This Dover edition, first published in 1981, is an unabridged
and corrected republication of the work first published in 1974
by Charles Scribner's Sons under the title *Knitter's Almanac.*

Wool and needles for all models supplied by Meg Swansen,
Route 1, Pittsville, Wisconsin 54466.

International Standard Book Number: 0-486-24178-5
Library of Congress Catalog Card Number: 81-67039

Manufactured in the United States of America
Dover Publications, Inc.
31 East 2nd Street, Mineola, N.Y. 11501

To the Unsure Knitter,
To the Blind Follower,
and
To all those who do not yet know
that they can design their own knitting,
this book
is encouragingly dedicated

Acknowledgements to Elinor Parker,
for kindness beyond the call of editorship,
to Tom Zimmermann, photographer,
and to sheep, who gave their wool.

Contents

JANUARY

An Aran Sweater

ONCE UPON A TIME there was an old woman who loved to knit. She lived with her Old Man in the middle of a woods in a curious one-room schoolhouse which was rather untidy, and full of wool.

Every so often as she sat knitting by the warm iron stove or under the dappled shade of the black birch, as the season might dictate, she would call out to her husband:

"Darling, I have unvented something," and would then go on to fill his patient ears with enthusiastic but highly unintelligible and esoteric gabble about knitting.

At last one day he said, "Darling, you ought to write a book."

"Old man," she said, "I think I will."

So she did.

It was well-received, but, although it contained much that was reasonable, and even new, it did not contain all the things she knew about knitting, nor any of those things she continued to "unvent." So she wrote another book, and you hold it in your hands right now . . .

IT IS QUITE TRUE; we do live in a schoolhouse in the middle of a woods. We have been in the United States since 1937, and we have three grown-up, beautiful, and intelligent children. One of them has two children.

I was born and brought up in England, in a middle-class family, and was educated by governesses and in private schools, which means that my head

1

contains some very odd pieces of information, indeed, and little formal knowl-edge.

My husband was born and *erzogen* in Bavaria, in a family of considerable culture, and had a good German education in proper schools and the Univer-sity.

For "brought up" and "erzogen" you may read "raised," but that always sounds to me like bread.

Our backgrounds and nationalities appear to complement each other nicely; we are now retired, and enjoying it exceedingly. He can carpenter, plumb, read, paint, write, brew beer, shoot, and fish. I can do none of these things except read and paint.

But I can knit. I knit all year, day in, day out. It is my passion, and I rarely knit the same thing twice the same way.

Here, then, is a knitter's almanac; a monthly record of the changing year in the light of my amiable craft. Let us start with a challenge—an Aran Sweater. Simpler projects will follow.

IT IS A COLD AND SNOWY JANUARY. The holidays are done with, and Twelfth Night will be any day now: what better time to embark on a long and lovely project? I have masses of thick unbleached natural cream wool, which with luck should work up into a really solid-looking Aran. It knits best at $3\frac{1}{2}$ stitches to $1''$, measured over stocking-stitch, and if you can find some wool which knits at the same GAUGE, we can work together.

Because I am thoughtful and kind, I will give directions for the same classic Aran at a GAUGE of 5 stitches to $1''$ (measured over stocking-stitch) at the end of the chapter, which means that I shall be making two sweaters while you make one, but it's all in the day's work, and a pleasure, I assure you.

For centuries Arans have been knitted by the womanfolk of the Western Isles of Ireland from the cream-colored, unbleached, handspun wool of their own sheep. Many of the jerseys have turtle-necks to keep out the wind, and $\frac{7}{8}$ sleeves that don't get wet and draggled when the nets are pulled in. Originally each family had its distinctive patterns, as the Scottish clans had their tartans. I don't know the reason for this in Scotland, but I have heard that the Aran family-patterns helped to identify the man washed up drowned. A sobering piece of common sense.

Some patterns were used by all families, but by now, what with loosely-knitted imitations from goodness-knows-where flooding the cheaper sweater market, the whole subject has become thoroughly confused.

Let us, therefore, design our own Aran, using the patterns that please us most. There are beautiful pattern-books available which contain many hundreds of different and distinct patterns in the Aran idiom. When you consider the combinations and permutations of so many possibilities, you can see that every knitter in the world could design a different sweater from various arrangements of these beautiful stitches.

Most Aran patterns are forms of cable, and all Aran sweaters contain several different ones. For ease of execution, I often divide my Arans into four, and put the same sequence of patterns in each quarter. You could, with only slightly more effort, divide *your* sweater in half, with the same pattern-sequence on back and on front. Or make a sampler of *all* different patterns, with the back different from the front.

Now pay close attention; the watchword for the next page or so will be GAUGE. What better way to start a book dealing with knitting?

GAUGE means the number of stitches—or, if necessary, fractions of a stitch—to 1″ in a given knitted article. Directions unfortunately often recommend a definite needle-size for this GAUGE. *Please, oh please* do not rely on this.

Take some of *your* wool and the size needle *your* intelligence tells you *might* be right, and *make a swatch*. That is to say, suit the needle-size to your own personal and peculiar way of knitting. Do NOT try to get 5 stitches to 1″ on a #8 needle if you have to work uncomfortably tightly to attain this GAUGE. It is my private opinion that a #8 needle is customarily recommended for 5 stitches to 1″ because it is physically impossible to knit at a finer GAUGE with it, no matter how you squeeze your stitches.

Some of us do not like to squeeze our stitches; we like to knit loosely and placidly. For a GAUGE of 5 stitches to 1″ we may need a #5 needle, and should use one. Experiment, for goodness' sake.

The foregoing, which I lay before you in all seriousness, and from the bottom of my heart, now brings us to the hitherto knotty problem of the GAUGE of Aran knitting.

Regrettably, many Aran directions call for a GAUGE of so and so many stitches to 1″ *measured over patterns.* This piece of doubtfully useful information belongs, if anywhere, at the end of directions; at the beginning it can lead only to muddle and possible sorrow. Are we supposed to cast on the full number of stitches, and, having completed several inches in patterns, and measured, find out that our knitting is too tight or too loose? We have very possibly been using the size needle recommended, our knitting tension is different from that of the knitter of the model, and this is the result.

When the original sweater was completed, the knitter probably laid it out flat, measured it, divided the number of stitches by the inches, and gave the result as the necessary GAUGE in pattern. How she arrived at the right number of stitches to cast on in the first place, it is perhaps kinder not to ask, as there is no easy way. Aran stitches, and all cables, pull in differently one from another, and if there are several patterns, all pulling in at various tightnesses, each will have a different GAUGE.

If, when the model was finished, the knitter had simply taken the same needles and wool, and worked up a small rectangle of stocking-stitch, and taken the GAUGE from that, we could do likewise, and match our stocking-stitch to hers. Then we would be in the clear for using the same needles and wool to make our Aran patterns at the same GAUGE as hers, and come out at least approximately right.

When you look at directions for an Aran, look also for the words "GAUGE measured over stocking-stitch," and you will save yourself grief. Should the directions say "GAUGE measured over patterns," proceed warily. Then it is a good idea to cast on half the stitches for the total body-width, and embark on an Aran cap instead of a swatch. Use all the patterns called for, and if the cap turns out to be exactly half the width of the intended sweater, you can start on this without a qualm, and be one cap to the good. Make it 6–8″ high, and bring it to some kind of a finish at the top. It is sure to fit somebody.

Should you realize that the cap is turning out narrower than half the wished-for width of the sweater, change to larger needles; your cap will be narrower at the lower edge, which is an advantage.

If it is wider than you want, change to smaller needles, and make it upside-down—that is, with the narrower piece for the lower edge. Cast off, knit up stitches along the cast-on edge, and finish *it* for the top.

Now you have a cap—or even two—some part of which is the correct GAUGE, and you can proceed with your sweater enjoying a feeling of confidence and rewarded intelligence.

There *is* a way of modifying a group of Aran patterns in a sweater without changing the needle (and thus the GAUGE), which I always bear in mind when working on a new design. I compute as best I can—drawing on experience, naturally—the number of stitches for half the sweater, and start the cap. (Isn't it convenient that a cap measures just about half a sweater?) Should the cap turn out narrower than I had hoped—shall we say by 2″—I add the necessary 2″ in the form of more purled stitches between the patterns. All true Arans have one or more purled stitches between their patterns. I reserve the right, and you can too, to decide on how many of them my sweater will have. If the GAUGE, measured over stocking-stitch, is $3\frac{1}{2}$ stitches to 1″, seven added stitches between patterns will yield two extra inches. If seven doesn't fit in too well, make it six, or eight; we will not quarrel with one stitch.

If my cap turns out too wide, I can take away some of the purled stitches between patterns, modify one of the patterns, or eliminate it entirely.

Let us cast on, then, for our experimental caps, anything between 90 stitches in thick wool and 100 or 110 stitches in finer wool, and forge ahead with the mental turnings and twistings which will result in a truly individual Aran, designed *by* you *for* you. Or for someone even dearer. You can take note of what I do, and do likewise; or improve on me.

Should you find these "Notes for Thinking Knitters" intimidating, look at the end of the chapter. There you will find exact directions for making this classic Aran, 44″ around, with more purled stitches between patterns, at a GAUGE—measured over stocking-stitch—of 5 stitches to 1″. Use any yarn that works up at this GAUGE. Unbleached cream all-wool is what *should* be used.

Fishtrap Pattern:

I took down Gladys Thompson's exemplary book "Patterns for Guernseys, Jerseys and Arans", the very first and best of the Aran books, which shows only classic and genuine Irish designs, and from it I chose two patterns. One is very wide; I shall put it twice on the front and twice on the back, and shall have little room left for much else, but never mind. It is an understated but rich pattern, and one of my favorites. As it has no name known to us, we call it "Fishtrap", because that is of what it reminds us. It will be flanked by narrow twisted-stitch cables; two of them to each quarter. The quarters will be divided by an absolutely minimal pattern—a vertical rib of just one twisted stitch (K 1 back). This stitch will run up both underarms and up the center of back and front. As I am planning a cardigan, I shall substitute K 1 B, P 2, K 1 B, at center-front, to allow for cutting.

Yes; I always cut cardigans, for I start them (and finish them, too, for that matter) as circular pullovers. Circular construction is especially desirable for Aran work, for it has it all over two-needle knitting when one is working complicated cables. If you have the right side of your knitting constantly under your eagle eye, you are much less likely to go astray with the patterns, and I think you will find the directions easier to read, too. I have arranged "Fishtrap" for you in columns, divided by its three vertical lines of K 1 B. Even if you tend to confuse the travelling-stitches, you will be able to use these vertical lines as guides. Between them, as you shall see, the travelling-stitches veer in several directions.

What is a "Travelling-Stitch"?

It is an essential but quite simple feature of many Aran designs, and is no more than a miniature two-stitch cable which edges its way to left or to right. If it is to travel to the left, it is achieved by Left Twist (LT); if it is to travel to the right, by Right Twist (RT). LT and RT are sometimes known as Back Twist (B tw) and Front Twist (F tw) respectively, as they are started from the back and from the front. I think that LT and RT are more expressive terms, and shall stick to them from now on.

A cable is usually made by taking two stitches on a spare needle and holding them in front of your work (Left Cable), or at the back of your work (Right Cable), while you knit the next two stitches. You then put the first two stitches back on the lefthand needle, and knit on. The two pairs of stitches have changed places, and you have effected a cable. Larger cables may be made in pairs of three, four, or even five stitches, or sometimes on uneven pairs of stitches. The smallest cable is made with two stitches, and this is the one that concerns us at the moment.

After the first few times of taking a single stitch on a spare needle, holding it in front or at the back while you knit the next stitch, and it trying to slide off all the time, the craythur, you will smartly come to the decision not to fool around with spare needles, but simply to knit the second stitch first and the first one second, and slide them both off the lefthand needle together. If you keep cabling the stitch in the same direction, it will start creeping across your knitting to become a full-blown Travelling Stitch. If you want it to travel to the Left, knit the second stitch from the back first; if to the Right, knit the second stitch from the front first. In short, perform Left Twist (LT) or Right Twist (RT) respectively. Here is how they go:

Left Twist:
Skip the first stitch on the needle, and dig into the second stitch from the back. Knit it, but do not take it off the needle. Now knit into the front of the first stitch, and slip them both off the needle together. LT completed. It leans to the *left*.

Right Twist:
I perform this differently from some knitters, and perhaps you will like this way too: Knit two stitches together from the front, but don't take them off the lefthand needle. Now dig into the second stitch, knit it again, and slip both stitches off the lefthand needle together. RT completed. It leans to the *right*, and is a good mirror-image of LT, even though performed in a rather unorthodox fashion.

The only other stitches you will need for "Fishtrap" are Knit (K), and Purl

(P) of course, and Knit 1 Back (K 1 B), knit into the back of the stitch, thus twisting it.

"Fishtrap" is 35 stitches wide and 28 rounds high, and I have given you a chart for it as well as conventional written-out instructions with the kind permission, nay, encouragement, of Barbara Walker. It is she who has collated and rationalized the disparate theories of charted knitting, and licked them into magnificent shape. Once you have tried complicated patterns, or even simple ones, from her charts, you will look only with pity on written-out directions.

The chart is as wide and as high as a single pattern-repeat. Start at the lower righthand corner and work your way across, following the symbols. A blank square is a Knit stitch; a dot is a Purl stitch. Where two diagonal lines run to the Left over two squares, make a Left Twist; where they run to the Right, make a Right Twist. The square with the B in it means "Knit 1 Back" (K 1 B); a twisted stitch.

Having, on a circular needle, of course, finished the execution of round 1 on the pattern-chart, complete the first round, putting in the other cables and the repeats of "Fishtrap", until you come to the first stitch of the round again. Then work round 2. And so on. Every pattern-round is shown, and every stitch. Notice that on the even-numbered rounds there are no twists: just knit and purl your way around. Don't forget the K 1 Bs.

A great advantage of this kind of chart is that it gives you a pretty good picture of the design you are aiming at. It has as many squares as there are stitches, and each stitch is in the correct relationship to its neighbors. Even if you insist on working from the written-out directions, check your progress with the chart. I'm willing to bet that you will finish up your Aran working from the chart alone.

Ribbed Cable:

This is the other pattern—a very expert-looking but deceptively simple cable of only five stitches, with a delightful piece of cheating on the cable-round. The only stitches you will need are Purl, K 1 B, and the cable itself, which is indicated by that long diagonal over 5 stitches. I made you cable right away on the second round because the closer the first cable is to the beginning of your work, the better off you are. You may even cable on the first round if you wish. Then, because the cable-pattern is 7 rounds high, and the "Fishtrap" 28 rounds, you can remember to work the cable on the 8th, the 15th, and 22nd and the 1st round of the large pattern.

Cabling every *seventh* round? you are saying; how *unusual!* Unusual, indeed, but one of the manoeuvres made possible by circular knitting. In two-needle knitting you must cable every 4th, 6th, 8th, or 10th row if you value your sanity. In circular knitting you can place your cables any distance apart that looks good to you. Actually, I worked a few of these cables eight rounds apart before I realized that the large pattern had 28 rounds, and that it would be convenient to have a cable-repeat that would divide into 28. It may sound silly, but the 7-round cables are prettier and more ropelike than the 8-round cable, which looks rather angular, efficient, and economical. Try it out, if you like, and see what you think.

The cable on the heavy cardigan, by the way, was worked the other way, Right over Left. Take your choice. Another small personal note is to the effect that I purled all 35 stitches of "Fishtrap" on the very first round on the 5 sts to 1″ pullover, to counteract the possible curling-up of such a large field of Knit stitches. This left me conveniently in the clear for working my cable-round on the *second* round, which was then the first round of "Fishtrap".

These, then, are our pattern-stitches; "Fishtrap" and "Ribbed Cable"; 35 stitches for the former, 5 stitches for the latter. If, for the cap, we cast on 100 stitches, it will allow for a "Fishtrap" on back and on front, with two "Ribbed Cables" on either side, which are separated by our tiny 1-stitch pattern of K 1 B. Each of these patterns will be separated by one purled stitch, so it comes out at exactly 100 stitches. Very neat.

All this I did, writing down and charting each stitch as I went along, and the result is quite a long and large "cap", 10″ across, 20″ around (perhaps a quite small cushion cover?!). If I double it, my sweater will be 40″ around, which happens to be just what I want. If I wanted more width, I would add some more purled stitches between the patterns. I have knitted a swatch of stocking-stitch with the same wool and needles, and its GAUGE is exactly $3\frac{1}{2}$ stitches to 1″, so for each extra 2″ needed I would insert 7 stitches somewhere between the patterns.

Now, with ill-concealed disapproval, I will compute the GAUGE of the cap in pattern. 100 stitches divided by 20″ is 5 stitches to 1″. An impressive-sounding statistic of, I believe, absolutely no practical value when one is embarking on an Aran project.

Achieve, then, a GAUGE of $10\frac{1}{2}$ stitches to 3″ ($3\frac{1}{2}$ stitches to 1″), measured over stocking-stitch, with the wool you plan to use, and we can knit together. If our stocking-stitch matches, our Aran patterns will match too.

While you are working, I shall not be idle. I will cast on 100 stitches once more, but this time with wool the thickness of knitting worsted, which knits up best at a smaller GAUGE—5 stitches to 1″, measured over stocking-stitch (5.45 sts to 1″ over pattern:)—for which I shall take a #4 needle. Do not be surprised if you need a larger or even a smaller needle-size. Work it out for yourself on the stocking-stitch swatch, then knit up a cap for proof.

HOW DID YOUR SWATCHCAP COME OUT? Mine, in the thinner wool (5 stitches to 1″, measured over stocking-stitch) on 100 stitches was 9″ across, or 18″ around: an average hat. Doubled, it would be just right for a sweater for a slender person who wears a 36″ sweater. If I want it to be 38″ around I will deploy about 10 extra stitches (2″) between my patterns. If I want a 40″, 42″, or a 44″ sweater I will add 20, 30, or 40 purl stitches, or even incorporate another small pattern in each quarter. The model shown has 40 extra stitches; 10 to each quarter. I inserted another minimal pattern of K 1 B each side between the "Fishtrap" and the "Ribbed Cable", and then added a second purl stitch between each pattern—a total of 10 added stitches per quarter, making 60 stitches in all per quarter, or a grand total of 240 stitches.

The simpler the shape of an Aran, the better—nothing should detract from the richness of the stitch-patterns. I usually make the body as a large tube, right up to the top. The slight shaping at the bottom of the one shown is caused by my having added the extra purl stitches between the patterns only after the first 3″ had been worked. I didn't do this on the cardigan, because

I counted on the garter-stitch border to "hold in" the lower edge.

When the body is the right length, cast off the front, and slope the back shoulder-line by casting off about 5 stitches at the beginning of each row until enough stitches remain for the back of the neck—about 6 or 7″ worth. You may like to incorporate a knitted-in, or Kangaroo-pouch neck-shaping. It goes roughly as follows:

About 3″ shy of desired body-length, put the center $\frac{1}{3}$ of the front stitches on a piece of wool, cast on 2 stitches, and continue working. When the body is finished as above, machine-stitch and cut the front center 3″, which will fall apart to reveal a nicely scooped-out neck.

Make the sleeves on a 16″ circular needle. Start at the wrist by casting on $\frac{1}{5}$ of the number of body-stitches. Join, and work around, starting patterns as on the body. I placed one "Fishtrap" running up the center of the sleeve, with the "seam" (one vertical line of K 1 B) diametrically opposed to it. Each side of the seam increase 1 stitch every 4th round, which will shape the sleeve to the correct width at its top. Background stitches are kept in purl, and soon there will be enough of them to fit in a "Ribbed Cable" each side of the seam if you wish. In fact this second pattern can easily be infiltrated, stitch by stitch, as the increases permit. This is all up to you, but don't complicate the undersleeve with too many patterns where they won't show anyway.

When the sleeve-length plus half the body-width equals the shirt-sleeve length of the wearer measured from neckbone to wristbone—allowing an inch or two for stretch—cast off, in pattern, with the strong hope that a cable-twist will place itself in the last round or so.

Now comes the cutting for the armholes. Baste a line down the upper sides of the body for the straight armholes, taking great care that they match the tops of the sleeves exactly. Machine-stitch (with a very small stitch) twice each side of the basting and across the narrow bottoms of the armholes, double-checking to be sure this is all at the right spot. Then—horrors—cut.

Shoulder-seams are sewn next, and sleeves pinned and sewn neatly in place from the right side. Cut edges of the armholes are pressed towards the sleeve inside, and whipped down with matching thread or fine wool. Pick up the stitches of neck-back and neck-front, knit up stitches from the sides (usually about 6–10) and work low, medium, or high turtle-neck in pattern. This may be cast off loosely, or faced back, or rolled over. In the latter case, remember to start working in the other direction somewhat less than halfway up, so that the turned-over pattern faces outwards.

The front of a cardigan is cut in the same way as the armholes, straight down the center. Border-stitches are picked up on a slightly smaller needle. from the right side, at the rate of 2 stitches for every 3 rows. Borders are worked in garter-stitch, quite firmly, for about 12 rows (6 ridges). Front-corners are mitred by increasing two stitches at these points every second row. (Lower border is worked separately, on 10% fewer stitches than were originally cast on.) Buttonholes are put in—seven on each side—at the halfway point of the border (see page 80). To calculate how many stitches to leave between them, do this:

Count the stitches of one front, subtract 6, divide the remainder by 6, and subtract 3 from the result. The number left will be the number of stitches between each of the seven 3-stitch buttonholes, with 3 extra stitches at the bottom. If you have a few stitches left over, fudge them away somewhere; nobody is going to count where you have 11 stitches between buttonholes and where 12 . . . Thus on the buttonhole row you knit 3, make a 3-stitch buttonhole, *knit the number of stitches you have calculated, make another buttonhole, and repeat from *. Sew buttons on the appropriate side for ♂ or ♀.

After all this I hope you will feel inspired to design, calculate, and execute your very own personal Aran, like unto nobody else's. Ambitious knitters may care to incorporate a raglan shoulder, or even a hybrid one, and in these cases it is a splendid idea to run a cable up the raglan-line, and decrease each side of it. Try anything that occurs to you—Arans are now your oyster; enjoy them.

So! I have Arans off my chest. The rest of the designs in this book will now seem childishly simple, and will, I hope, have the appeal of a child—a nice child; not too pretty, not too prissy, but with good genes and reasonable upbringing.

PITHY DIRECTIONS FOR THE ARAN PULLOVER

GAUGE: 5 sts to 1″, measured over stocking-stitch.

SIZES: 38″, 40″, 42″, 44″.

MATERIALS: 7 4 oz skeins of 2-ply Sheepswool, or 6–7 4 oz skeins of any yarn yielding the above GAUGE. 1 24″, 1 16″ circular needle of a size to give this GAUGE (size 4–size 8).

BODY: With 24″ needle cast on 216 sts. Join, being careful not to twist, and work around. Establish patterns as follows:

*K 1 B, P 1, Ribbed Cable (5 sts), P 1, K 1 B, P 1, Fishtrap (35 sts), P 1, K 1 B, P 1, Ribbed Cable, P 1. Rep from * 4 times in all. (4 × 54 sts = 216 sts.) Place marker at first st, and between patterns if wished. Work straight for $3\frac{1}{2}$″. Inc. now for size you wish by inserting P sts between patterns:

8 sts for 40″. (224 sts in all)

16 sts for 42″. (232 sts in all)

24 sts for 44″. (240 sts in all)

(The exigencies of the design called for a slight modification of figures from the basic ones given in the text.)

Work straight to 26″ or desired length to shoulder. Cast off front half, leaving center 40 sts on piece of wool. On back work back-and-forth, casting off 5 sts at beg. of each row until 40 sts remain, which are put on a piece of wool.

SLEEVE: Cast on 42 (44, 46, 48) sts on the 16″ needle. Join, and work around, establishing Fishtrap pattern at center. Mark 1st st of round for underarm and here establish a vertical line of K 1 B. Inc. 1 st each side of this rib every 4th rnd. When sleeve-length + half of body-width equal shirtsleeve length of wearer, (allowing $1\frac{1}{2}$–2″ for stretch), cast off. Most sleeves are about 18″ long.

Baste Straight Armholes at top of body-sides to match sleeve-tops exactly. Machine-stitch twice with small stitch each side of basting and across bottom of armhole. Cut on basting. Sew shoulder-seams. Sew in sleeves, hemming them neatly from the right side. Neaten cut edges inside towards sleeves.

Knit Up Neck-stitches on 16″ circular needle, and work as wanted. For working details, see text.

Written out Directions for "Ribbed Cable":

5 sts wide, 7 rnds high.

Rnd 1. Knit 1 Back twice, P 1, Knit 1 Back twice.

Rnd 2. Cable rnd. Take first 3 sts on spare needle and hold in back of work. Knit 1 Back twice, from the spare needle K 1, Knit 1 Back twice.

Rnds 3–7. Repeat rnd 1.

Written out Directions for "Fishtrap" Pattern:
35 sts wide, 28 rnds high.

Rnd 1. (LT) 4X,	K1B, (RT) 4X	K1B, (LT) 4X,	K1B, (RT) 4X.
Rnd 2. (P1, K1) 4X,	K1B, (K1, P1) 4X	K1B, (P1, K1) 4X,	K1B, (K1, P1) 4X.
Rnd 3. P1, (LT) 3X, P1,	K1B, P1, (RT) 3X, K1,	K1B, K1, (LT) 3X, P1,	K1B, P1, (RT) 3X, P1.
Rnd 4. P2, (K1, P1) 3X,	K1B, (P1, K1) 4X,	K1B, (K1, P1) 4X,	K1B, (P1, K1) 3X, P2.
Rnd 5. P2, (LT) 3X,	K1B, (RT) 4X,	K1B, (LT) 4X,	K1B, (RT) 3X, P2.
Rnd 6. P3, (K1, P1) 2X, K1,	K1B, (K1, P1) 4X,	K1B, (P1, K1) 4X,	K1B, (K1, P1) 3X, P2.
Rnd 7. P3, (LT) 2X, P1,	K1B, P1, (RT) 3X, K1,	K1B, K1, (LT) 3X, P1,	K1B, P1, (RT) 2X, P3.
Rnd 8. P4, (K1, P1) 2X,	K1B, (P1, K1) 4X,	K1B, (K1, P1) 4X,	K1B, (P1, K1) 2X, P4.
Rnd 9. P4, (LT) 2X,	K1B, (RT) 4X,	K1B, (LT) 4X,	K1B, (RT) 2X, P4.
Rnd 10. P5, K1, P1, K1,	K1B, (K1, P1) 4X,	K1B, (P1, K1) 4X,	K1B, K1, P1, K1, P5.
Rnd 11. P5, LT, P1,	K1B, P1, (RT) 3X, K1,	K1B, K1, (LT) 3X, P1,	K1B, P1, RT, P5.
Rnd 12. P6, K1, P1,	K1B, (P1, K1) 4X,	K1B, (K1, P1) 4X,	K1B, P1, K1, P6.
Rnd 13. P6, LT,	K1B, (RT) 4X,	K1B, (LT) 4X,	K1B, RT, P6.
Rnd 14. P7, K1,	K1B, (K1, P1) 4X,	K1B, (P1, K1) 4X,	K1B, K1, P7.
Rnd 15. P6, RT,	K1B, LT, P1, (RT) 2X, K1,	K1B, K1, (LT) 2X, P1, RT,	K1B, LT, P6.
Rnd 16. P6, K1, P1,	K1B, (P1, K1) 4X,	K1B, (K1, P1) 4X,	K1B, P1, K1, P6.
Rnd 17. P5, RT, K1,	K1B, K1, LT, K1, (RT) 2X,	K1B, (LT) 2X, K1, RT, K1,	K1B, K1, LT, P5.
Rnd 18. P5, K1, P1, K1,	K1B, (K1, P1) 4X,	K1B (P1, K1) 4X,	K1B, K1, P1, K1, P5.
Rnd 19. P4, (RT) 2X,	K1B, (LT) 2X, P1, RT, K1,	K1B, K1, LT, P1, (RT) 2X,	K1B, (LT) 2X, P4.
Rnd 20. P4, (K1, P1) 2X,	K1B, (P1, K1) 4X,	K1B, (K1, P1) 4X,	K1B, (P1, K1) 2X, P4.
Rnd 21. P3, (RT) 2X, K1,	K1B, K1, (LT) 2X, P1, RT,	K1B, LT, P1, (RT) 2X, K1,	K1B, K1, (LT) 2X, P3.
Rnd 22. P3, (K1, P1) 2X, K1,	K1B, (K1, P1) 4X,	K1B, (P1, K1) 4X,	K1B, (K1, P1) 3X, P2.
Rnd 23. P2, (RT) 3X,	K1B, (LT) 3X, P1, K1,	K1B, K1, P1, (RT) 3X,	K1B, (LT) 3X, P2.
Rnd 24. P2, (K1, P1) 3X,	K1B, (P1, K1) 4X,	K1B, (K1, P1) 4X,	K1B, (P1, K1) 3X, P2.
Rnd 25. P1, (RT) 3X, K1,	K1B, K1, (LT) 3X, P1,	K1B, P1, (RT) 3X, K1,	K1B, K1, (LT) 3X, P1.
Rnd 26. (P1, K1) 4X,	K1B, (P1, K1) 4X,	K1B, (P1, K1) 4X,	K1B, (K1, P1) 4X.
Rnd 27. (RT) 4X,	K1B, (LT) 4X,	K1B, (RT) 4X,	K1B, (LT) 4X.
Rnd 28. (K1, P1) 4X,	K1B, (P1, K1) 4X,	K1B, (K1, P1) 4X,	K1B (P1, K1) 4X.

X = times. Directions in parentheses are to be repeated as many times as specified. K = knit. P = purl. LT = Left Twist. RT = Right twist. K1B = knit into back of st.

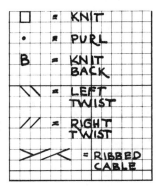

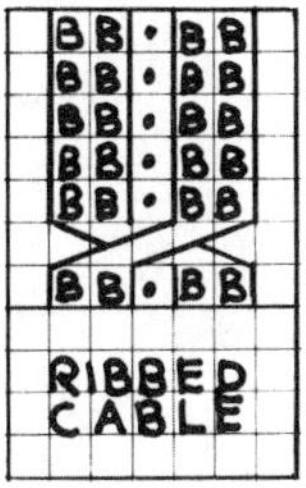

Ribbed Cable chart (top left):

B	B	•	B	B
B	B	•	B	B
B	B	•	B	B
B	B	•	B	B
B	B	•	B	B
B	B	•	B	B

RIBBED CABLE

Legend:

□ = KNIT

• = PURL

B = KNIT BACK

╲╲ = LEFT TWIST

╱╱ = RIGHT TWIST

╳ = RIBBED CABLE

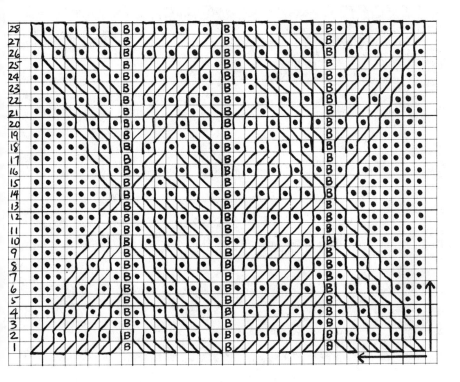

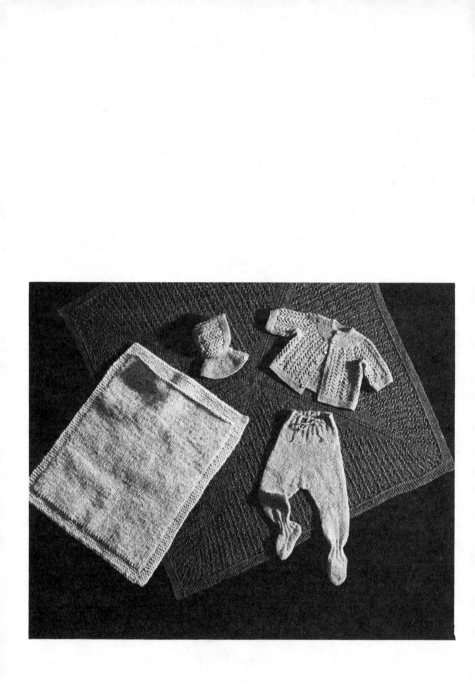

FEBRUARY

Some Babies' Things

ALTHOUGH BABIES RARELY, if ever, express their pleasure at being dressed in wool, it is surely manifest when you dote on a small plump person soundly and contentedly asleep, swaddled in woollen sweater, woollen leggings, and a soft wool bonnet, snugly tucked under a fine warm wool blanket.

Nothing keeps a baby as warm and comfortable as wool; even when damp, let alone wringing wet, wool doesn't become chilly, and to many of us it is well worth the trouble of washing carefully.

If there is one fact on which all grandmothers agree, it is that no daughter-in-law knows how to wash wool. This may be true, but it is no reason for the grandmas to stop knitting. Do they expect their handmade offerings to be carefully preserved in layers of tissue-paper and never worn? They have perhaps forgotten how often baby things have to be washed. The baby surely doesn't mind if they do become a little shrunken and yellowed. Let the grandmas keep up the supply of soft woolies, and avert their minds' eye from the ultimate fate of their knitting—at least it is being used.

Here is a practical suggestion: make baby things in darker and less delicate colors, so that they visit the washtub less often. A soft heather-grey outfit is well-suited to a baby's complexion, especially if you incorporate some white around the edge of the bonnet. You can line it with white and have the lining show around the border, or edge it with white knitted lace. Navy blue looks good on a baby, with touches of pale blue or silver-grey. A fiercely blue-eyed child in a greenish blue Shetland cap is a sight to be seen. And what's wrong with scarlet?

These colors, of course, will hardly be available in baby-wool, which even at its most dashing doesn't venture beyond delicate green and pale yellow, but there's no law against dressing a baby in any wool you see fit, as long as it is soft and of good quality.

Pass by the synthetic yarn department, then, with your nose in the air. Should a clerk come out with the remark that All Young Mothers In This Day and Age (why can't they save their breath and say "now"?) insist on a yarn which can be machine-washed and machine-dried, come back at her with the reply that one day, you suppose, they will develop a baby that can be machine-washed and -dried.

Babies—and people generally—have been dressed in wool since around the beginning of history. Even as comparatively recently as my own youth I can remember neither the word, nor the phenomenon, of wool-allergy. A minimal minority wriggled their way through my boarding-school days complaining of scratchy underwear, but they outgrew the sensitivity—they had to. I believe that the dressing of babies in the very softest wool, automatically and naturally immunizes them against any allergy to it. If you start a child off with synthetics, you will have no one to thank but yourself if it has to pass its days in cheerless plastic-yarn sweaters, cut off from the warmth and comfort of wool.

If I were stuck with a child allergic to wool I would become very sneaky: I would make it a sweater of orlon or whatever, into which I would knit one color-pattern of wool. If this were received and worn without carping comment, I would increase the dose—next sweater, two patterns, next one, three. After twenty sweaters—in theory, at least—I would have a nice normal wool-wearing child. At least I would have tried. If caught at my fell deed, I could always say that the particular color I wanted was only available in wool.

For older children allergic to wool I would make an absolutely stunning sweater—the sweater to end them all—but in wool. Having observed young people for a couple of generations, and seen them go through all manner of fashion-tortures without batting an eye, right down to the current exposure of bare blue shivering shanks in winter, I know that they can and will endure all manner of discomfort in order to wear what they want to wear.

LET US CONSIDER the most useful things to knit for a warmly-dressed baby. As in the previous chapter, and throughout the book, concise and business-like directions for all projects described are given at the end of the chapter.

We will start with a blanket—a simple oblong one with an unusual working, which affords soothing and mindless knitting. It is also a growing laprobe, so if your baby is being born in the summer, better make the blanket quite early in the game.

It is based on the great and simple principle of Double Knitting. Double Knitting (as distinct from English "double knitting", which is their name for knitting worsted) always seems to me, though fascinating, a great waste of time. It is the procedure of working back-and-forth on two needles in such a manner as to produce a circular piece of fabric. On the first row you alternately knit and slip the stitches; on the next row you knit the stitches you slipped, and slip those you knitted. Thus each stitch is handled twice, once to be slipped and once to be knitted. These two rows are repeated on an even number of stitches, and the result is a rather charming tube of stocking-stitch, which occasionally sticks together where you made a mistake, and which, in unskilled hands, may have an erratic edge.

I would much rather—and faster—take a circular needle to this job, complete it sooner, and avoid those stuck-together bits.

The knitting public, however, is intrigued by Double Knitting, so, as one of its members, you shall be given Double Knitting.

Never one to waste time and effort, I have tried to incorporate four advantages, to make the undertaking worth while.

First, Double Knitting is for some reason very light, relative to its bulk, and soft as a cloud if you make it in light, thick wool (as it might be Sheepsdown) with large needles. It makes a splendid pad when you lay the baby down on the hard floor for its kicking exercises.

Second, it is the warmest of covers—warm as two blankets, which, of course, it is.

Third, I have given it a handsome and functional border of garter-stitch all around. It starts with four ridges of this.

If I had cast on sufficient stitches for the lower edge to accommodate the (double) number necessary for Double Knitting, I would have had a wavy lower and upper border. I'm too old a fox to be caught by that one. I cast on *half* the number of stitches, worked the lower border in garter-stitch, and for the first row of the pattern I *made* the necessary extra stitches by backward loops over the righthand needle. Thus instead of slipping alternate stitches on the first pattern-row, I manufactured them, increasing by M 1. (See p. 141)

The end-result is a springy cloudlike blanket, held in on all four sides by a severe and dignified band of garter-stitch, which gives it body, and at the same time tames the customary erratic edges.

Knit up a sample on about 20 stitches, or any even number, and use it to decide on how many stitches you need for the size you want, be it pad, baby-buggy robe, or crib-blanket. Make the borders the width you personally prefer, remembering to work as many ridges (2 rows each) at the bottom and top as there are stitches on the side-borders. Skip the borders of the 5th and 6th, the 11th and 12th, and 17th and 18th rows, and so on. Just turn short of the border-stitches, and work back, for two rows. You don't *have* to do this, but I think you'll find it worth the trouble, as the side-edges will hold in better this way. If you make your sample a square, you will gain a bonus of a handsome and useful hotpad or pot-handler.

DOUBLE-KNITTING POT-HANDLER

With very thick wool and about #10½ needles cast on 20 stitches. Work 4 ridges of garter-stitch. Next row: K 4, *K 1, Make 1 by backward loop over righthand needle. Repeat from * until 4 stitches remain, ending with Make 1, K 4. (32 sts) Next row; K 4, *K 1, wool forward, slip 1 as if to purl. Repeat from * to last 4 stitches, K 4. Repeat this row for as long as necessary. Then K 4, *K 2 together, repeat from * to last 4 stitches, K 4. Work 4 ridges of garter-stitch and cast off.

I mentioned four advantages. The fourth is the fact that if you don't knit those stitches together on the last pattern-row, but bind off front and back separately, your blanket, when you make it, will also serve as a snug baby bag.

SQUARE SHAWL

Now TRY A SHAWL. This has a beginning, but no end, as it may be stopped whenever you please, depending on time, patience, and wool-supply.

Start at the center on five needles. These are more practical than four needles, as you will have one for each quarter of the square shawl, and one to knit with. If one of them is a slightly different size, it *doesn't matter*. It will be a sliding and slippery business to start with, but will soon settle down. Some people even like to work the first six to eight rows on two needles, and sew the seam later and fairly invisibly. Suit yourself; I like to do the job properly, and start with Emily Ocker's circular beginning on 8 stitches. This you will find in the Appendix. Emily says she didn't invent it, but I've never heard of it before. She says it is of German origin.

On the eight stitches knit 1 round. Next round, Wool over, K 1, around (16 stitches; 4 on each needle). Knit 1 round. Next round: *Knit 1, wool over, Knit one, wool over, Knit to end of needle. Repeat from * on the other three needles.

If you want a very plain, beautiful, simple shawl, keep repeating the last two rounds. On every second round you will be increasing two stitches at the beginning of each needle, and there will of course be one more stitch at the beginning of each needle each increase-round. This 8-stitch increase every second round will produce a square shawl which lies flat. The spaces between the increases will naturally become larger and larger, and the stitches more and more numerous, so that soon you can put them on a 16″ circular needle, and then a 24″ one. The 24″ needle can see you through the whole project, but some knitters like to progress to even longer ones, from 27″ up to a limit of 48″—my word, what a snake.

When the work is on the circular needle, be sure to mark your increase-points, using a special marker for the first one of the round. For a shawl I prefer loops of brightly-colored wool, safety-pins, and ring-markers, in that order.

Now you are only human, and early in the shawl those areas of plain knitting between the increases will begin to appear somewhat bland and you will start thinking of embellishments.

Put in a pattern, by all means, the lacier and more open, the better; this is after all, a shawl. Just be careful to center your patterns, and keep their number of stitches constant. I like to work a single repeat of a pattern in each quarter, to start with. Then, when sufficient stitches have been increased, I will place a repeat each side of this, and so on. The small steps formed by the increased stitches, waiting until their number suffices for a complete pattern, are pleasant and pretty, so I never fool with blending the patterns into the corners, where they might tangle with my increases and cause disaster.

When choosing a pattern, pick one which directs you to purl back on alternate rows in two-needle knitting, which means that on a circular needle you will knit the alternate rounds.

Need I say that I arrange to have the working rounds of the pattern (the rounds with the Overs, the K 2 togs, the SSKs, and all the excitement) the same as those with the four corner-increases. Then every second round is a mindless and relaxing one of knitting all the stitches and all the Overs.

For the edge of the shawl try a sideways garter-stitch border as described in the Appendix. A cast-off edge is difficult of achievement and often tight and distressing in appearance and use.

Block all shawls severely. Dampen them (wash them if necessary), blot or spin out all possible moisture with towels or in the wash-machine, and block them on a large bed, sticking pins through the edges into the bed at close intervals. You can also block them on the rug, putting down a sheet first if you are that kind of housekeeper. If you wish, you can stretch them quite ferociously with each pin about 2–3″ apart, to achieve an edge that looks as though it had been knitted in points.

When the shawl is quite dry, fold it so that it keeps its shape. For each washing follow the same procedure.

YESTERDAY WAS A GOOD DAY. There was a big ski-jumping meet at Westby, not far from here, where, tucked away in one of the steep narrow West Wisconsin valleys, and efficiently managed by the local ski-club, there is the highest jump in the U.S. Stop—I'm a liar; it's the second-highest now.

It was a perfect and very cold day, and we travelled by devious and little-known roads. Arriving before noon, we immediately indulged in a festive picnic in the car, garnished with a bottle of the best beer, and another of Rhine wine. Amazing how a couple of bottles lend style to an occasion—when backed by suitable glass and mug—in a way which a Thermos can never emulate. Several of the best linen tea-towels help, too, as well as a small board so arranged that it will lie level between the two guzzlers. From there on store cheese, hardboils, hardtack, and apples can easily complete the picture, with little expense of time, money, or energy.

Jumping started punctually, and the Old Man disappeared in the direction of the take-off, where he could keep matters under his expert eye. The sun blazed through the windshield, my legs were wrapped in the old knitted blanket, and in spite of grand resolutions to take down all the distances jumped and get some knitting done in the intervals, the Rhine wine had its effect and I slipped off into the most delightful post-prandial nap. My special technique for car-cat-naps is to sit bolt upright, and let the chin drop down as far as it can on the chest, relaxing all neck-muscles. My reflexes are now so conditioned that this pose sends me to sleep almost immediately; the head doesn't loll, the mouth doesn't open degradingly, and I like to think that there is no snoring, although the family is in a conspiracy to tell me that I always snore, which is plain nonsense.

The beeping of horns at some particularly spectacular jump woke me up, and I was conscious and knitting in time to welcome back the Old Man, highly pleased with his day of spectator-sport. Believe me, in the days—so-called "good old"—when he jumped himself, there were no naps for me; just tremble-tremble.

I did get some knitting done during the drive there and back, however, as I had taken along the baby-jacket on which I am currently working. Its yoke and part of a sleeve were done by the time we arrived home to be welcomed by two ecstatic cats and the stove with ashes still glowing.

I am trying to simplify and rationalize the traditional two-needle baby sweater, and tame it with percentages. To reduce its seams to a minimum I started at the top, with a garter-stitch yoke. When the necessary increasing was finished, I changed to the pattern-stitch, and worked straight to the underarms, where it is divided as follows:

Right Front:	15%,	plus 4 border-stitches (or more, if you wish).
Right Sleeve:	20%.	
Back:	30%.	
Left Sleeve:	20%.	
Left Front:	15%,	plus 4 border-stitches (or more, if you wish).
= a neat	100%,	plus 8 border-stitches (or more, if you wish).

Then the sleeves are worked. They have 7 stitches cast on at each end and are finished with a border of garter-stitch. Lastly back and both fronts plus 14 stitches picked up at each underarm are worked together for as long as desired, and finished with a similar border. Result: a beguiling baby-sweater with only two seams to sew. Make it in any color or weight of wool you like, or happen to have handy. Yoke and borders in garter-stitch or seed-stitch will not curl; garter-stitch is really more practical, as it will absorb the yoke-increases with less fuss. Put buttonholes down either or both fronts at regular intervals.

The yoke-increasing gave me a hard time, causing much scribbling on backs of envelopes, until the Old Man rescued me with one stroke of his pencil. Use 140, he said, and your sleeve- and body-percentages will fit in perfectly. And they do, even down to each one being a multiple of seven. This dictates that any stitch-pattern used should have a 7-stitch repeat, and I know of a couple of pretty ones that qualify. For the neck I had cast on 42 stitches (plus 8 stitches for the borders). Did you know that 42 can be increased to 140 in three easy steps of K 2, M 1, across? After the first increase-row you will have 63 stitches, after the second, 94, and after the third, 141 stitches. One stitch too many, you will say quickly. Well; nothing is perfect; just don't increase that last stitch. Full directions for 140-stitch jacket at end of chapter.

I am making a bonnet with the same wool and pattern as the jacket, and shall surely finish it off with booties to match. Babies rarely appear in fashion-coordinated clothes, but it's not from want of receiving sets from grandmas.

This bonnet is dedicated to keeping the neck warm. Why bother the baby with a clumsy scarf knotted around its neck when you can knit an extension to a bonnet? Make any bonnet you please, of the type which encloses the ears, and buttons under the chin. When it is finished, knit up all stitches around the lower edge, and make a spreading collar, which will lie flat around the neck and over the shoulders, and be kept in place under the sweater or jacket. Increase at a slower rate than you used for the yoke of the sweater; perhaps 7 increases, evenly-spaced, every second row. Keep at it until you are sick and tired. The longer it is, the warmer the baby, but don't make it wider than the shoulders.

WE WILL NOW PASS on to longies, or baby-leggings.

I first saw this practical baby-garment in Germany, when I was a girl, and I used them for my own children, who were born in the U.S. We lived in those days in coldwater flats and houses (coldwater being a euphemism for just plain *cold*), so conditions were quite European. Longies take the place, in one fell swoop, of all manner of dresses, soakers, and booties, and let the child wriggle to its heart's content, unimpeded, and without uncovering itself.

With grandchildren in the offing, I went into longie-knitting again, and designed my own peculiar version. They are made by formula, so no matter what wool you use, or what GAUGE, if you stick to the shaping the result is in proportion.

Some knitters are hamstrung by superstition, which tells them that the shaping of knitting varies according to the thickness of the wool and the GAUGE. The *size* does, but the *shaping* does *not*. In good plain stocking-stitch, if you want an angle of 45° you increase (or decrease, as the case may be) at the rate of one stitch every second row or round. If you do this *every* row or round, the shaping will be twice as fast, at an angle of $22\frac{1}{2}$°, or so I am told. Decreasing 2 or 3 stitches every row (naturally at the beginning or end) will give you a faster decrease still.

If you want a very slight shaping, eliminate (or increase) one stitch every third or fourth row. The angle remains constant, no matter what your GAUGE. If you want to narrow or widen your work by one inch, add or subtract as many stitches as your GAUGE gives you to 1″; the rate of shaping will give you the angle it inherently *has* to give you, no matter what wool you use.

The above is quite true, and once you believe it, you will find home-designing of knitting easier than you could possibly imagine.

For longies, therefore, I cast on sufficiently for the waist, and work a piece of ribbing. I shape the back by working short rows back and forth across increasingly more and more stitches, until I hit the side-seams, or the places where the side-seams would be if I were fool enough to make longies in pieces, on two needles. Soon I start to increase, fore and aft, at the rate of two stitches every third round, for the baby's bottom. When the length warrants it I put 5 of the stitches, also fore and aft, on pieces of wool, for the crotch; these will later be woven together. Cast them off, if you hate and fear weaving, but consult the Appendix first. Hate and fear do you no good, and weaving is fun, and easy. Each leg is then continued separately on sock-needles. (There are such things as 11″ and 9″ circular needles, which would work for legs, but I find them far less convenient to manipulate than sock-needles.)

I decrease at the inseams, at the same rate of 2 stitches every third round, until I have a reasonable width for the leg, and then again at the infant calf, if I am in a jocund mood. As I approach the foot I switch to K 2, P 2, ribbing for two or three inches, as this is a good clinging stitch for the ankle. I finish off with a bootie-foot or a sock-foot, as whim dictates.

Some of the larger longies are still being worn by the two-year-old, with many darns at the knees, and with shoes. The smaller ones have come in useful for the second baby, and because I am a truthful woman, I must admit that some of them are made in half-wool and half-nylon. They are wearing magnificently, but have become stringy. It depends on what you want for your baby—all-wool and comfort or half-wool and durability. Now I think about it, if we'd had our wits about us, we would have incorporated nylon in all knees and feet.

Our favorite longies are those on which we used up odd remnants of wool. A green pair has a cute grey color-pattern at the calf, and then becomes steel-grey for the feet. A navy pair has a white pattern at the knees and scarlet calves and feet. They must be actually seen on young legs for their true charm to become apparent.

Thrift and conservation are in the wind: how delightful to find that using up wool-remains improves the appearance of finished product.

You know, if our ancestors had thrown out their furniture every decade, as we do, where would we go for antiques? Let us give some thought to the well-being and enjoyment of our descendants, patch up our *lares* and *penates*, and hang on to them, so that the future will inherit at least some relics of our heedless and wasteful age. Working over something, and repairing it,—whether we re-finish furniture, fix over an old house, or put new cuffs on a sweater—not only gives things new life and makes them look cared-for, but embeds them still deeper in our affections.

PITHY DIRECTIONS:
DOUBLE-KNITTING BLANKET OR PAD 20″ × 26″.

GAUGE: 10 sts to 4″; $2\frac{1}{2}$ sts to 1″, measured over completed fabric.

MATERIALS: 4 4oz skeins Sheepsdown, or 4–5 skeins of any thick wool to give the above GAUGE. 1 pr needles to give *you* this GAUGE, #$10\frac{1}{2}$ or larger.

Cast on 54 sts. K 8 rows (4 ridges garter-st.) Next row: K 4,*(K 1, Make 1), Rep from* to last 4 sts, K 4. (100 sts). Start pattern, slipping all first sts:

Row 1. K 4, *K 1, wool fwd, sl 1 as if to P, Rep from * to last 4 sts, K 4.

Rows 2,3,&4: Rep row 1.

Row 5. Rep row 1 to last 4 sts, turn.

Row 6. *K 1, wool fwd, sl 1 as if to P. Rep from * to last 4 sts, turn. Rep from * in 1st row, and keep repeating these 6 rows until piece is 24″ long. Next row: K 4, K 2 tog (or ssk) to last 4 sts, K 4. (or cast off the back-sts) K 8 rows and cast off,

SHAWL 43″ × 43″

GAUGE: 4 sts to 1″, measured over stocking-stitch.

MATERIALS: 10 oz Shetland wool, or similar yarn which gives the above GAUGE when knitted loosely. 1 16″, 1 24″ circular needle, 1 set of 5 dp needles of a size to give *you* above GAUGE. (sizes 5–8). 1 crochet-hook.

Cast on 8 sts by Emily Ocker's method as described in Appendix. Put 2 sts on each of 4 needles, and work with the 5th. K 1 rnd. Next rnd YO, K 1, around. (16 sts). K 1 rnd.

Rnd 1. K 1, YO, K 1, YO, K to end of each needle. (24 sts). Rnd 2 and all even-numbered rnds, K.

Rnd 3. K 2, YO, K 1, YO, K to end of each needle. (32 sts).

Rnd 5. K 3, YO, K 1, YO, K to end of each needle, and so on, increasing 2 sts on each needle every 2nd round. At 64 sts transfer to 16″ circular needle, placing markers at each increase-point. At 104 sts transfer to 24″ needle. Place patterns as desired, centering carefully. At about 21″ or around 800 sts, stop knitting, having omitted the corner-increases for the last 1½″. Add 7 st garter-stitch sideways edge (see Appendix), mitering it slightly at the corners by working K 6, turn, K back. K 5, turn, K back. K 4, turn, K back, K 5, turn, K back, K 6, turn, K back, continue with border. Weave end to beginning.

BABY SWEATER ON TWO NEEDLES; PRACTICALLY SEAMLESS

GAUGE: About 5 sts to 1″, but babies come in various sizes.

MATERIALS: 3 oz Shetland wool or other baby yarn. 1 pr needles of a size to give *you* above GAUGE. (approx. sizes 2–5)

Cast on 50 sts and work in garter-stitch. Work 4 ridges (8 rows). Next row: K 4, *K 2, M 1. Rep from * to last 4 sts. K 4. (71 sts) Work 4 ridges. Repeat inc. row and 4 ridges (102 sts). Rep inc. row, omitting 1 inc. (148 sts). Change to pattern, keeping first and last 4 sts in garter-stitch and putting in buttonholes (Y O, K 2 tog) about every 8th ridge. At 4½″, work 25 sts, then work back-and-forth on the next 28 sts (plus 7 sts cast on at each end of them; 42 sts in all) for about 4″ for sleeve, ending with 1″ of garter-stitch.

Repeat for second sleeve. Place remaining 92 sts on needle, knitting up 4 × 7 sts at the cast-on sleeve-sts, and continue with pattern and border for 5″, or to desired length. Decrease 10% (K 8, K 2 tog across) and finish with 1″ of garter-stitch. Cast off loosely, in P, on the right side. Sew sleeves.

Gull Pattern for Baby Sweater:

7 stitches wide; 4 rows high:
Row 1. (Wrong side) and all other wrong-side rows—Purl
Row 2. K 1, k 2 tog, YO, k 1, YO ssk, k 1. Repeat across.
Row 4. K 2 tog, YO, k 3, YO, ssk. Repeat across. Repeat from row 1.

BABY LEGGINGS

GAUGE AND MATERIALS: Same as previous design. Don't worry too much about size; babies vary, and knitting stretches. 1 16″ circular needle, and 1 set sock-needles of the same size.

Cast on 84 sts on the 16″ needle. Join, and work around in K 2, p 2, for 3 rnds. Next rnd: K 2, YO, P 2 tog around for eyelets. Rib 10 more rnds.

SHAPE BACK: Starting at center-back, K 5, turn, p 10, turn, k 15, turn, and so on until you have p 40, turn. Work even in stocking-st for 24 rnds. Mark 3 sts at center-back and -front.

SHAPE FOR HIP: Inc 1 st each side of marked sts every 3rd rnd. At 126 sts work even for 5 rnds. Put 5 sts at center-back and -front on pieces of wool, and complete legs separately on sock-needles.

LEG: Work around on 58 sts and dec 2 at inseam every 3rd rnd (K 2 tog, k 1, ssk). At 46 sts work even for 20 rnds. Mark center-back, and dec. 2 sts here every 3rd rnd until 36 sts remain. Rib for 15 rnds, or to desired length to ankle.

BOOTEE-FOOT: On 14 sts at center-front make *Instep.* Row 1. sl 1, k 12, p 1. Row 2. Sl 1, k 2, p 8, k 2, p 1. Work these 2 rows 10 times. Knit up 11 sts along sides of this piece and continue around in stocking-st for 10 rnds. On last rnd K 2 tog 4 times at toe and heel. Take out needles, fold flat, and weave sides. Weave the pair of 5 sts at crotch tog. (For cute shorts, cast off after the first 5 rnds of leg.)

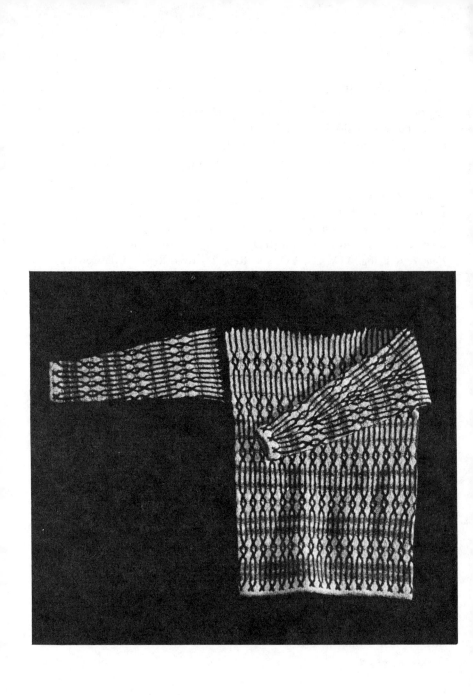

MARCH

Difficult Sweater (Not Really)

A KNITTERS' QUESTION which arises perennially is, "How much wool shall I buy?" To this question there is no blanket-answer, but several qualified ones:

If you are using very thick wool, buy more than you could possibly imagine; if you are using very thin wool, buy surprisingly little.

The rule of thumb is that five or six 4 oz skeins of knitting worsted is about right for the average adult sweater; that is, 20 to 24 ounces. A really massive sweater, in giant wool, at perhaps $2\frac{1}{2}$ stitches to 1″, may take two pounds of wool, or even more. If you are using Shetland (or any wool of comparable thinness, knitting up at around 6 stitches to 1″) you can usually get away with 10 ounces for an average sweater.

And when I say Shetland, I mean study the label carefully. If it admits to enfolding a yarn of only 5% Shetland, even its manufacturer must agree that it is hardly Shetland at all, and should not be counted as such. It is also sometimes quite a bit thicker than real Shetland.

Real Shetland wool is a truly exclusive product, as it *has* to come from a cluster of small islands off the north coast of Scotland, and these islands have room for only a limited number of their special sheep. The wool is spun at 2-ply, finely, very finely, and very finely indeed—almost of cobweb fineness. The most usually found is the first of these three, which should be worked at a GAUGE of 6 stitches to 1″, or even more tightly if you wish. It yields a soft, lightweight and economical fabric.

The whole matter of quantity of wool boils down in part to the observance of our old friend GAUGE. If you are going to use a thick wool at a large GAUGE, you will need more by weight than if you are planning a finely-knitted sweater at a small GAUGE. Thus if cost enters into the picture for you, remember that although fine wool may cost more per ounce than thick wool, a thin sweater nearly always costs less than a thick one, because the wool goes so much further.

Some imponderables are the way you knit, and the kind of clothes you like. A tightly-knitted garment takes more wool than a loosely-knitted one, as the fabric will be denser. Sweaters for people who like their things long and wide are naturally going to take more material than for those who like their things short and skintight. A ski-sweater with color-patterns takes more wool than a plain one—how *much* more depends on the incidence of patterns. A light-weight lace-patterned sweater at a large GAUGE takes the least wool of all.

Have I covered everything? The best answer I can give, then, is threefold:

1. Ask the sales clerk. She has a horror of selling you too little, as she well knows the headaches that can ensue from running short. She also has a vested interest in making a good sale, which fact is often pleasantly qualified by a willingness to take back leftover skeins, if neat and clean, within a reasonable length of time. *Preserve your Sales-slip.*

2. Keep a little book in which you enter details of every project you complete: kind of wool; GAUGE; amount of wool; final measurements; reaction of recipient; years of wear. Your book will be of signal help when you embark on a new project.

3. Buy too much wool. As I told you, wool shops are very understanding about surplus skeins. Better find out, though, just how understanding they plan to be. If you do have wool left over, do not despond. It can go into your wool-drawer and wait for many future uses: borders, color-patterns, small socks and mittens, even mending. Or needlepoint and crewel embroidery. Perhaps the most gratifying use is in a large casserole afghan, in which you can show your skill and inventiveness by employing numberless different patterns, colors, and weights of wool. Thin wools may be doubled or trebled to make them conform approximately to the general GAUGE; thick ones may be split for the same purpose.

What do you do if you run short of wool and cannot match it? You can do one of several things, some of which entail ripping, but ripping in a good cause. If you are in doubt at the beginning as to the sufficiency of the wool:

1. Make the sleeves last. Divide the remaining wool for them in half, and make $\frac{3}{4}$ sleeves if necessary.

2. Plan a circular sweater from the bottom up. If there is not enough wool for the yoke, make it in a different color, or with many color patterns. The method is suitable for round or raglan yokes.

3. Plan a sweater from the neck down, and finish the lower borders in a different color, or with color patterns.

If running short comes as a rude surprise, there are several little dodges you may like to try:

1. Make all borders of a different color. Take out the lower body-ribbing (see p. 146), use the wool gained to finish the shoulder, or whatever, and add ribbing of a different color.

2. Make the sleeves of a different color, with cuffs of the main color.

3. Blend in wool of a pretty good match by working 2″ of alternate rows of the two shades.

4. Use your ingenuity, and invent another dodge. I would be happy to know of it, and pass it on, as this problem crops up all the time, and with nearly everybody.

TODAY IS STUBBORN-COLD, 20° below at 11 this morning, but I am as stubborn as the winter, and still insist on enjoying the white landscape. I am about to keep myself busy, happy, and occupied, by taking you through the workings of what I like to call my Difficult Sweater. It isn't really, but it entails a new trick, which I have yet to notice in any sweater I have ever met. I call it, rather baldly, "Travelling Color-Pattern".

Regular ski-sweater and Fair Isle color-patterns are beautiful and fascinating, and rewarding to execute, but they are sometimes rather angular, as their diagonals slope in a series of small steps. The eye compensates for this; it is a knitting convention, and a handsome one. Why, though, should it be the end of the road for knitters who wish to give their patterns a more flowing line?

Flowing lines are commonly seen in textured knitting-patterns, and particularly in Travelling-Stitch, typical of Aran designs. Shall we make a colored Travelling-Stitch on a differently-colored background? We shall.

We will start with a cap, on a multiple of 6 stitches—say 90, or 96, or even 102 of them. For a design we will take one which appeared on the dust-jacket of a previous opus about which I have had many pitiful enquiries. I had loaded the photographer with all the knitted artifacts on which I could conveniently lay hands, and he bore them off to his ivory tower, to return surprisingly soon with the beautiful shot for the cover of "Knitting Without Tears". Naturally, all the sweaters he used couldn't be incorporated in the book, and no one has resented this, but that pink-and-Loden-green pullover at the lower lefthand corner fascinated many knitters, so here are the directions.

Its shape is the simplest (straight tube for body; tapered tubes for sleeves, which are cast off straight and sewed into straight cut armholes) and the pattern is much simpler than it looks. Let us practice it on a cap.

Vertical lines of single dark-green stitches, two stitches apart, run up a coppery-rose background. They approach each other in pairs, by the simple device of decreasing and making stitches, and cross, thus:

Work one round of 1 green, 2 pink to get yourself started. On the next round, with the first green stitch, in green, SSK (or, if you like, sl 1, K 1, psso), to consume the pink stitch to its left. Before you, you have a pink stitch and a green stitch. Knit them together with the green wool. The two green stitches now touch, and you have eliminated two pink stitches. This elimination is compensated for by making one pink stitch each side of the green stitches with a pink backward loop over the righthand needle. In directions this reads: M 1 pink, SSK green, K 2 tog green, M 1 pink, K 2 pink. Repeat this around.

On the next round, one green stitch is crossed over its green neighbor by Left Twist, as in Travelling-Stitch, or Baby Cable. Thus: *go behind the first green stitch, knit the second green stitch, knit the first green stitch, slip both stitches off needle together. Knit 4 pink stitches, and repeat from * around.

The green lines have crossed, and will now diverge again, by reversing the first process. *When you come to within 1 stitch of the first crossing, K 2 together (a pink stitch and a green stitch) in green. Make one pink stitch (one only) and SSK in green with the second green stitch and the pink one beyond it. Knit 2 pink stitches, and repeat from * around. Yes; you have increased only one pink stitch instead of two, but if you make two stitches next to each other in one round it is unsightly. The second pink stitch is increased between the two green stitches in the following round: *K 1 green, K 1 pink, M 1 pink, K 1 green, K 2 pink. Repeat from * around.

How often you cross and re-cross the lines is up to you. If you like, you need never cross these particular ones again, but let them slope away, to right and to left, crossing all other green lines in their path, and forming an elegant diamond pattern.

However, in this particular pattern the pairs of green lines keep crossing and re-crossing each other, after long intervals of fifteen rounds and short intervals of three rounds. I had considered this to form a species of vertical trellis, but it strikes an Important Member of the Family as being similar to a suit of chainmail, so the final title is "Chainmail Sweater".

Having a devious mind, I hadn't worked more than an inch or so of the prototype before I started considering how to vary the background color to soften the trellis effect. One round after completing the first crossover I changed the copper-pink background to cranberry red, and, my devious mind going full bat, decided that by blending the two colors between the trellises but not within them I could make them stand out better.

There are several ways of blending two colors in knitting: they may be used on alternate rounds, they may be used for alternate stitches, or they may be joined by a purled row on a stocking-stitch fabric.

The third choice is my favorite at the moment. It is not original; I picked it off the Bohus sweaters from Sweden. These sweaters were the product of a strictly-conducted, magnificently-directed cottage industry, and were of great fineness, perfect execution, and incredibly beautiful design in muted colors. They had been evolved by a master designer-craftswoman who used natural colors of beige and grey for the body of the sweater, and decorated lower borders, cuffs, and yokes with a mixture of wools and angora in small intricate designs, employing both knit and purl stitches. So skillfully did she blend her wools and stitches that the designs would be difficult, indeed, to copy. I hasten to add that I have no intention of doing this. If there's one thing I despise, it is "designing" by copying, or even by adapting someone else's design. But to be inspired by a new and admirable technique? I have no law against this; we wouldn't get far if we spent all our time in our ivory (or woolen) towers.

I took an old design of my own; a very simple pattern employing a strict sequence of three stitches of one color and one of another, varied by occasional plain rounds. I gave this pattern different colors, and further enlivened it by regularly-sequenced purled stitches. It was transformed, and I learned a great deal.

A purled stitch makes a bump; we all know that; but a purled stitch in a different color makes a bump of the old color with a modest V of the new color below it. Thus the sequence of a vertical stitch-row reads: fabric of old color, one stitch of new color, one bump of old color, and away on into the new color. It pulls the new color down into the old, and pushes the old color up into the new; it interlocks the colors. This is hard to describe, as you may have noticed. Try it for yourself and see. Experiment with it, and you will notice that by skillful employment of colors and an occasional purl stitch you can produce the impression of having worked a round with three colors at once, while in actuality you have used only two.

To blend colors, then, work an occasional stitch of purl (in the new color) in the first round in which the new color is introduced.

To give variety to texture, work purl stitches, or blocks of purl stitches, in stocking-stitch fabric; vertical lines of purl will recede; horizontal lines will stand out. Combine the two techniques of color-blending and texture-difference and see what happens. Try to write it down as you do it; sometimes it is not too easy to see what your particular genius was up to in a given pattern after you have finished it!

When I am graphing a design of this type I use symbols—cross, dot, diagonal line, etc.—for the different colors, and a plain square for the main, or background color. When a stitch is purled, I superimpose a horizontal line across the square.

There is a sad ending to my Bohus story—the beautiful sweaters are no longer to be had, as they were too expensive for the cheapskate tourist trade.

Now the fishermen's wives, who helped their grocery-money during a period of depression by knitting for a fair wage, are again scuffling. Or perhaps not; let us hope that times have improved, and that they now knit for themselves.

ARE YOU ENJOYING YOUR CHAINMAIL CAP? How are your criss-crosses? Is the background color being varied?

After finishing the first crossing on my sweater I had 15 rounds to play about with before I started my second crossing, and this is where I decided to vary the background again. The first two rounds were in the pale color, the next five in the darker red, the center round in the pale color, then five more dark red rounds, and two more pale ones. Then it was time to cross again. Each time I changed background color I purled the two stitches between the pairs of green stitches on the first round of the new color; thus the color-transitions within the trellises were smooth, and those between them somewhat speckled. The result was pleasing. I made the second crossing, worked one round even, changing the background color to red, complete with purled stitches, and then crossed again.

Now there was a horizontal row of long trellises with fifteen rounds between crossings, and a row of short trellises with only one round for its center. I decided to stick with this sequence—alternate spaces of fifteen rounds and one round between crossings.

Perhaps you can imagine that as I started the second long trellis I decided upon a slight variation. . . . I worked only four rounds of dark red, with three pale rounds in the center. At the next long trellis I diminished the dark area to three rounds, and increased the central pale area to five rounds. I don't think I have to go through the rest of this litany, do I? You can see the results on the sweater and will notice that the last long trellis finished up very neatly with no deep red at all. But excitement mounted, to say the least, as I approached my favorite sweater-length of 27″, wondering if the pattern would come out even. . . Yes; I know that I could have found out by measurement and counting, but there would have been no suspense that way. I much prefer to hold my breath, and knit and see.

Self-control was rewarded; the completed sweater is exactly $26\frac{1}{2}''$ long. I could have added one more small trellis at the shoulder, but decided against it, thinking it might look fussy. Perhaps you will decide *for* it.

The sleeves were great fun.

As this was to be a drop-shouldered sweater, with no armhole-shaping—just vertical cuts to match the width of the straight sleeve-tops—the sleeves were to be increased regularly, two stitches every fourth round, starting at the wrists. For them one-fifth of the body-width was cast on—48 stitches; exactly 8 trellises. (The body had had 240 stitches; 40 trellises.) At the fourth round the trellis had just been started, so I increased one stitch neatly by "M 1" (backward loop over R needle) each side of the first trellis. At which point I thought let's have a little game; let's keep this first trellis as the underarm line, and increase each side of it every fourth round, keeping the increases in pattern.

I did this, and was utterly rewarded. That underarm shaping is something to be seen; the regular increases cause other trellises to sprout from the original center one like nothing so much as a great tropical plant. All increases were formed by "M 1" in whatever color wool was at the moment indicated. I swear I won't be able to graph it; you must just do as I say, studying the photograph with a magnifying-glass. I must admit that I worked both sleeves at once, so carried away did I become, and so great was my apprehension of having my beautiful sleeves vary by so much as one stitch, one from the other.

When both sleeves were the right length (roughly 18″, depending on the wearer) I topped them off with a scant inch of trellis-green and laid them out to be considered.

Right then I abolished the term "underarm seamline" in this particular case—this masterpiece of increasing wasn't about to be banished to the ano-nymity of the underarm; this was going to be a superb embellishment of the back of the sleeve, where it could be admired by all.

I had some doubt whether the sleeve would lie properly in such an un-orthodox position—after all, it was at a slight angle—but the steam-iron melted away my doubts and the slight angle with a few puffs. In a docile fashion the angle straightened itself, and the sleeves were sewn in. The increasing formed an elegantly decorated line running up the sleeve at the back, from the back of the wrist to the middle of the armhole.

Have no illusions as to this being a blatantly obvious piece of styling, but the eye of the true knitter, behind this sweater in the towline, will gleam, the lips will move soundlessly, and the hands reach for some kind of paper and pencil. Who knows but that comments, questions, and a beautiful friendship will be the result?

WE ARE IN MILWAUKEE BRIEFLY, to see the play, and to take care of other errands for which the big city is better than the provinces. I hate to admit this, but it is true.

The trip produced one important knitting note—for me, at least. We went to the last day of the annual Designer-Craftsmen Show at the University, where two of my ponchos were exhibited.

Of course I played it real cool; sauntering, absorbed, from exhibit to exhibit, but my eye kept sliding ahead of me—*Where* are my ponchos? *How* do they look? My word, some of these exhibits are very wild, indeed, and will show up my poor little knitted efforts.

Knitting is almost an orphan among accepted crafts, such as potting, weaving, and metal-work, and only a few shows contain knitted pieces. Too long has the word knitting suggested pot-handlers, Girl Scout squares, booties, and rather lumpy, if loving, sweaters. By these has it been typed in the public's—and sometimes the jury's—consciousness. I see no reason why well-designed and well-made knitted pieces shouldn't take their place among other fabrics, and this is the end towards which I strive. Sometimes I am hoist with my own petard, as when an entry of mine was disqualified because a similar one had appeared in one of the knitting magazines. How could the jury guess that the sweater in the magazine was also mine?

Anyway, I finally, and, I hope casually, came upon my ponchos, in some very high class company indeed. They looked all right. In fact they looked warm, pretty, and beguiling; so beguiling, in sooth, that on the card of the Blacksheep one there was a small red spot.

SOLD!

Happy Easter.

PITHY DIRECTIONS FOR CHAINMAIL SWEATER

GAUGE: 5 sts to 1″ measured over stocking-st. 6 sts to 1″ measured over pattern, which pulls in. *Make a swatch cap first.*

SIZE: 40″ around. For each 1″ more of less desired width, add or subtract 6 sts.

MATERIALS: In 1-ply "Homespun," or knitting worsted, 4 4 oz skeins Light (Lt), 2 skeins Dark (Dk), 1 skein Medium (Med) color. Light and Medium should harmonize, but Dark not necessarily. 1 16″, 1 24″ circular needle of a size to give *you* correct GAUGE.

Cast on 240 sts in Lt on 24″ needle. Join, and K around for 2 rnds.

START PATTERN, which is 6 sts wide and 25 rnds high:

Rnd 1. K 1 Dk. K 2 Lt. Rep. around.

Rnd 2. SSK (p. 141), Dk, K 2 tog Dk, M 1 Lt, K 2 Lt, M 1 Lt. Rep. around.

Rnd 3. K 2nd Dk st from back, then 1st Dk st, slip both off needle tog, K 4 Lt. Rep. around.

Rnd 4. One st before Dk st K 2 tog Dk, M 1 Lt, SSK, Dk, K 2 Lt. Rep. around. (Each pattern-repeat will have only 5 sts.)

Rnd 5. K 1 Dk, K 1 Lt, M 1 Lt, K 1 Dk, K 2 Lt. Rep. around. (6 sts again.)

Rnd 6. Rep. rnd 1.

Rnd 7. K 1 Dk, K 2 Med, K 1 Dk, P 2 Med. Rep. around.

Rnds 8–11. K 1 Dk, K 2 Med. Rep. around.

Rnd 12. K 1 Dk, K 2 Lt, K 1 Dk, P 2 Lt. Rep. around.

Rnds 13–17. Rep. rnd 8.

Rnd 18. Rep. rnd 12.

Rnds 19 & 20. Rep. rnd 1.

Rnds 21–24. Rep rnds 2–5.

Rnd 25. Rep. rnd 7. Pattern complete. Rep. from rnd 1. You may prefer to enlarge the single Lt rnd in center of long Trellis to 3, 5, 7, and 9 rnds successively, and let the Med. rnds gradually disappear. Continue pattern until piece measures $26\frac{1}{2}″$ or to desired length finishing with 3 rnds of Dk. Cast off.

SLEEVE: with 16″ needle cast on 48 sts or $\frac{1}{5}$ of body-sts. Work pattern as on body, increasing 2 sts at underarm every 4th rnd. At $17\frac{1}{2}″$ or desired sleeve length, work 3 rnds Dk and cast off.

Measure straight armhole to match sleeve top exactly and run basting-thread. With small machine-stitch, stitch twice each side of basting and across bottom. Cut on basting. Sew about ⅓ of top for each shoulder. Lap sleeves over armholes and hem in place on right side. Press raw edges inside towards sleeve and whip flat. Knit up all sts around neck and work facing for 1½″, increasing 2 sts at *each* end *every* rnd. Do not cast off, but fold hem under and stitch down lightly. For hems at cuffs and lower edge, knit up all sts in Med. P 1 rnd, K 1 rnd. Decr 10% by K 8, K 2 tog around. When hem is 1½″ long sew down lightly without casting off.

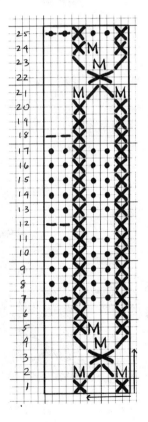

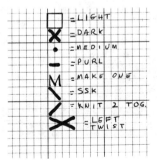

APRIL

Mystery Blanket:
Weaving

THIS YEAR, snow is still with us for at least the first part of April, and I am cheering myself by designing a blanket, on the theory that if I keep my thoughts firmly fixed on winter and warm woollies spring will be a pleasant surprise.

A blanket is proving educational and startling. For a long time I have brooded on a fabric of identical squares sewn together, and have expressed benign interest in all such artifacts, from granny afghans to large elaborate cotton bedspreads with raised leaves, chunks of reverse-stocking-stitch, and embossings of bobbles. From the beginning it had occurred to me that if the squares were started at the center and not cast off, their sides could be woven together to produce the mysterious effect of the blanket having been knitted in all directions at once. I bedded down this brainwave in my subconscious, and have allowed my life to simmer along until now. Now squares have gripped me, and perhaps they will grip you too.

Squares form a particularly convenient spring and summer project; they are of a good size for carrying around, and are repetitive in the extreme, well-suited to jumpy knitting. After the first three or four are made you start insisting yourself into a state of stitch-perfection, and a good thing too. When joining begins, uneven numbers of stitches to be picked up or woven can be irritating, and may betray the inscrutable construction of your knitting.

Perhaps many people share with me great pride in producing a piece of work which will cause their expert friends to exclaim, "*How* did you *do* it?" at which they can sit back with smug and satisfied smiles, and gradually, with hints and winks, give out clues.

Much of my knitting is given over to techniques to foil friends. For instance I often cast off by the casting-on method (see Appendix), and cast on by the invisible method so that stitches can be picked up and cast off, or knitted in the reverse direction (Appendix again). One ruse which I have yet to employ—although I mull it over slyly—is to take out the casting-on and deliberately and rather clumsily put in old-fashioned casting-off. Perhaps I will never do this; it is unethical to deceive deliberately and gratuitously. When deceit, however, leads to a better-looking result, let the devil take the hindmost.

The square I chose was the plainest; regular stocking-stitch, started at the middle, and increased with yarn-overs, two at each of the four corners, every second round. I well knew that if I made elaborate squares, encrusted with knobs and excrescences, and riddled with lace-patterns, I would keep wanting to embellish and improve as I made each one, and end up with a set of muddled and possibly uneven squares. The essence of the project, too, was speed; I wanted to get the thing done to see if it worked. I chose 4-ply Sheepswool, which knits up at a GAUGE of 3 stitches to 1″, and ensures great speed of execution, as well as a thick, warm, heavy blanket.

I started with 8 stitches deployed on four #10½ needles (see Appendix under Emily Ocker). This was awkward going for the first few rounds, but at the fast rate of increase—8 stitches every second round—in no time there were 32 stitches, which would fit on a 16″ circular needle. At this point I put a marker at the beginning of the round; in fact I put two markers—a palpable metal one in the form of a safety-pin, and a flexible one in the form of a circle of different-colored and finer wool, which transfers more easily from the left to the right needle. The safety-pin was soon left behind, as my fingers rarely failed to feel the woolen marker as it came moving along. A trap into which I fell only occasionally was the tendency to knit into the marker itself when I was knitting and reading at the same time.

Some may gasp and stretch their eyes, but knitting and reading at the same time is just a matter of practice. Of course you must love knitting and you must enjoy reading; if you don't love them equally, one at a time is sufficient.

Before our children could read we established the regular and laudable habit of reading aloud to them after supper. After a few years of reading what *they* wanted—frequently rather bland and unpalatable stuff—we made the rule of not reading a book aloud that we didn't enjoy ourselves, which cut out horse-stories, comics, and Dick-and-Jane maunderings. Before long the children started to share our taste in books, and both parents, the reader and the listener, enjoyed themselves more. We were able to infiltrate books which in no way qualified as children's fare, but which, read with care, edified and entertained all hands. In fact we sometimes had trouble finding the book when reading-time started, because someone had sneaked it upstairs to puzzle through, and get the jump on the next installment.

Perhaps this is one reason why we have produced a trio of reading young. One thing I do know; it is much easier to form a habit in children if the parents are already addicted.

Anyway, during the period of having to read, aloud and repeatedly, extremely dull books, I trained myself to knit at the same time, in order to keep awake. It didn't take long. A good reader-aloud's eye is always at least half a line ahead of his tongue (and sometimes, when Bowdlerization is called for, a couple of lines). The time taken for the tongue to catch up with the eye was usually enough for a stitch to be picked up or new wool joined in. When more complicated difficulties arose, the family just had to wait a few minutes.

Start practising therefore, and your new skill will be acquired more quickly than you would think possible, but train yourself first by knitting with your eyes shut, and then by reading to yourself while knitting.

THERE I WAS, then, with 32 stitches on a 16″ needle. The whole square could have been made on this needle, but the stitches would have become quite crowded, and a 24″ needle is easier to manipulate anyway. You may transfer to it at 64 stitches at this large GAUGE. In fact if you don't own a 16″ needle, you can use four needles up to 64 stitches. In this case, I prefer to knit like a Frenchwoman, with five needles, so that each quarter section has a needle to itself.

Keep careful count of the stitches; there should be exactly the same uneven number of them in each quarter, separated by the four single corner-stitches. On the increase-rounds make a yarn-over (yo) on either side of each corner-stitch; on the in-between rounds just knit into the loops made by the yarn-overs. You will find that you have a charming line of double holes running diagonally up each corner of your square.

When there are 96 stitches (four quarters of 23 stitches separated by the four corner-stitches), say to yourself, as I did, this is nearly enough.

Then I said to myself, and perhaps you will too, why bother to go on increasing. My square is pretty big; another three or four rounds should finish it. If I work them without increasing I may get some interesting results, and at least the corners will be rounded, which is a desirable thing in a knitted corner.

I celebrated the completion of the increasing by purling one round. After four more knit rounds I put all the stitches on pieces of wool, and tore into the making of more squares, so that I could start weaving them together. All this is leading up to:

WEAVING

If you are one who hates and fears weaving (or grafting, or—why?—Kitchener-stitch), and tries to con others into doing it for you, now is the time to take yourself in hand.

First, be assured that this blanket contains more weaving than you would believe possible. Second, be doubly assured that weaving, when you have really learned to do it, and are in possession of a good large blunt weaving-needle, is more fun than needlepoint. It is a talent to be gloried in; wait no longer to acquire it. It is *much* less complicated than other things you have learned, such as golf, or how to wash glasses properly, or Philosophy, or how to organize a Formal Wedding. It may be that weaving is less necessary than these, but it crops up frequently in knitting, and is at least worth the trouble of examining closely. Once examined closely it will reveal itself to be simple in the extreme.

Start by teaching yourself properly. It is easier if you avoid weaving with the stitches on two needles and the slip-as-if-to-purl-leave-stitch-on-needle routine. Make yourself, instead, a pair of practice-samplers.

With thick wool and a firm GAUGE, cast on about 20 stitches. By thick wool I don't mean knitting worsted unless there is nothing thicker handy. It pays to buy a hank of rug-wool, or even rug-cotton, so that you will be learning on something solid. Work about 4 rows of garter-stitch (all knit) and then change to stocking-stitch (K 1 row, P 1 row, as if you didn't know). If you like you can make a neat edge by knitting the last stitch of every row, and slipping the first stitch as if to knit, pulling the wool firmly. (Might as well learn a useful border while you're at it.) When there are about six rows of stocking-stitch, break the wool, and take the piece off the needle. Make another piece. Gently steam the stitches so that they turn and face the front. Now go to the sewing-machine and carefully run two rows of machine-stitching along the second-from-last row of knitting, so that both this row and the last row of loose stitches worked into it are firmly fastened down. If you get nervous, you may run more rows of stitching. If you have no machine, hold down the stitches with hand-stitching, employing backstitch. If you don't know what backstitch is, ask your grandmother, or somebody's.

There you are, now, with two fine, durable, useful, weaving-samplers, in less than an hour, even including chasing after grandmas. I have about a dozen pairs, which live quietly in their box between trips to knitting-groups. Each pair is provided with a stout piece of butcher's twine and a *very large, very blunt needle with big grooves at the eye-end;* big enough to grasp, quick to thread, and groovy enough to ease the wool pleasantly along without bunching. Have I emphasized my opinions on weaving-needles strongly enough? I hope so.

Now you are going to weave, *in* the flat, *on* your knee, with stitches that can neither *drop* nor *run,* and with a strong case of amnesia on the subject of anything you already know about weaving.

Thread the needle with butcher's twine.

Lay the two pieces of knitting on your knee, smooth side up, with the loose stitches facing each other horizontally. Work from right to left. With the blunt needle, go *down* through the first stitch on the lower piece (nearest you) and *up* through the second stitch. Pull the string through, leaving a *3″* tail. Repeat this on the first two stitches of the upper piece, leaving, of course, no tail. Now put the needle *down* through the second stitch on the lower piece (the stitch you came *up* through last time), and *up* through the third stitch. Repeat this on the upper piece.

You are weaving. Repeat the above process on stitch after stitch until you arrive at the end of your samplers. Adjust the tension by tightening the stitches (or, rarely, loosening them) until they are indistinguishable from those of the two pieces of fabric which they unite.

Admire your handiwork, grasp the piece of twine firmly, and pull it out, so that the samplers separate again. Weave again, and again, like the young lady from Spain, until the movements of your hands and needle are automatic. You are now in the powerful position of a knitter able to teach other knitters to weave.

Soon ambition will egg you on to attempt to weave garter-stitch, and even pattern-stitches. Garter-stitch weaving may be practiced on the stocking-stitch samplers, by putting the needle *down* and *up* through the lower piece, and *up* and *down* through the upper piece, to form a line of purled stitches. When performing this feat on a piece of garter-stitch fabric, be sure that the last row of the lower piece is purled, and the last row on the upper piece smoothly knitted. This is hard to explain; refer to the drawing in the Appendix.

Weaving a pattern-stitch can be the very devil, and can only be done perfectly when the knitting-grain of both pieces runs in the same direction. Both knit and purl techniques have to be combined, and if you are determined to do it, refer to "Mary Thomas's Knitting Book" under "Grafting, ribbed."

I hope that after practicing weaving on the samplers you can achieve it with confidence, because as soon as you have four blanket-squares finished you will be itching to see what they look like when joined. I was, anyway, and right away I wove them, 19 stitches of one side to 19 stitches of another, leaving

5 stitches at each corner for final finishing. Thus, when the four squares were woven together to form a large square, there remained 20 stitches at its center, five from each of the center corners of the four squares. These I picked up on four needles, and purled for one round. I knitted two more rounds, then knitted 2 together around (10 stitches). The wool was broken, threaded through the ten, and finished off. The four holes which then became apparent were neatened with the weaving-threads and some ingenuity.

The result pleased me highly. I may add that it was not achieved without considerable trial and error, but the joins were adequately concealed, and if one weren't aware that the sides of the squares had been woven, it would have been a puzzler to know which way the grain of the knitting had run.

Very quickly making squares became quite automatic, as they knitted up so fast. If I sat at it, I could make one in an hour. They measured about $10\frac{1}{2}''$ square, so I decided on a blanket 4 squares by 6—24 squares. My word!—a day and a night for a whole blanket, working non-stop! As a child I heard of a Victorian bedspread-knitting lady who started to knit in her sleep, and that was when her husband put his foot down.

Of course I joined as I went along; a good thing too, as the $3''$ tails I had originally left at the ends of the weaving proved too short, and I learned to leave at least $6''$. (Are you thrifty about each inch of wool, as I am? I have a neurotic fear of running short at the end of a project by just the length of wool I might hastily waste at the beginning.)

The larger the blanket became, the more I tended to use it for the taking of naps, and was thus in an excellent position to corroborate my decision that four squares by six was just right.

In practically no time at all it was finished, and woven together, and the 15 small four-corner joinings accomplished by the aid of my set of large clacking sock-needles.

Then came the reward, the sour cream on the potato soup, the last step; the borders.

I had been hoping that they would scallop themselves, and, sure enough, they did. As the last five rounds of the squares had had no increasings, the centers had tended to hump themselves up. When the humps were flattened, the corners had naturally rounded themselves, and along the edges of the blanket there were dimples, with scallops between. Fine. Along the borders, therefore, I wove the squares together right up to the single corner-stitches, picked up all stitches along one side, and worked six ridges of garter-stitch. In order to miter the corners I increased one stitch at the beginning of each row by knitting twice into every first stitch. This was for the short side, on 96 stitches. The next side was a long one, on 144 stitches; easier to work on two 24″ circular needles. (Wind stout rubber bands around the unused ends, so that the stitches don't slide off.) On this second side I increased one stitch at the beginning of the row only on one end; on the other I knitted into the end-stitches I had increased on the first side. The third section was treated in the same way, and on the fourth I knitted into the miter-stitches at each end. Thus all four corners were mitered. You may make them separately and sew them if you like.

Casting-off? Need you ask. Of course I cast off by the casting-on method (see Appendix) which would fool anyone into believing that the thing had been started around the outer edges. Then I blocked it with dabs of the steam-iron. The borders wanted to pull in somewhat, which is a fault in the right direction. They can always be coaxed out in blocking. The reverse is not true. Once a border had made up its mind to stretch, and to become what can only be described as frilly and wavy, there is little to be done but take it out and knit it again. It *can* be coaxed in, but it won't stay coaxed.

To increase the inscrutability of this blanket, omit the purled rounds.

PITHY DIRECTIONS FOR BLANKET 45″ × 66″.

GAUGE 3 sts to 1″.

MATERIALS: 11 4 oz skeins 4-ply Sheepswool, 1 16″, 1 24″, 1 set sock-needles of a size to give you approximate GAUGE.

Cast on 8 sts on 4 needles and work with a fifth one. K 1 rnd. Mark first st on each needle and increase by yo each side of it every second round. (8 increases for 2 rounds) Change to 16″ needle at 32 sts and to 24″ needle at 64 sts. At 96 sts, work 1 purl rnd and then 4 knit rnds without increasing. Place sts on 4 pieces of wool, 1 for each side. Make 24 squares. Weave center 19 sts of sides together (at sides of blanket weave right to the corners). Pick up 20 sts where the 4 corners meet. P 1 rnd, K 2 rnds, K 2 tog around. Thread wool through the 10 sts and finish off. Rep. for 15 joinings in all.

BORDERS: Pick up sts of one side, and work 6 ridges of garter-st, increasing 1 st at beginning of each row for miter. Rep. on other 3 sides. Sew corners. Block. Sneak under, and take well-deserved snooze.

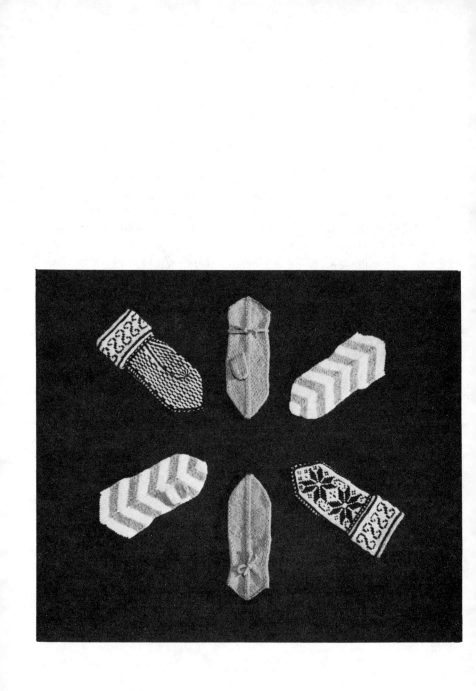

MAY

Mittens for Next Winter

IT IS BETTER NOT TO MAKE MITTENS IN A HURRY. When snow flies and small frozen hands beg for warmth (sob), the actual knitting tends to be perfunctory and possibly scamped; one economizes on the number of stitches; one does not make the cuffs sufficiently long. The main object then is to turn out scads of mittens to appease the demand, and enjoyment of production is not what it might be.

Let's make them in May; let's take our time over them; let's venture into new approaches and designs; let's enjoy them. For the compulsive knitter, hot weather need not put a crimp in his or her activity. Large projects may lie heavy and warm on the lap, but small things like mittens and socks are easy to carry about outdoors, and can be made surprisingly fast. Stash them away as they are finished, and when the time comes, next winter, you can deal them out with a liberal hand.

Keep in mind the saddening fact that mittens lose themselves in wear, especially the smaller sizes. Try making them to be interchangeable for right or left hand. This is quite easy to do by knitting the thumbs to stick out at the sides, instead of from the palm. Don't even worry about from where the thumb springs until you come to the decreasing for the finger-tips. At this point, arrange your decreasing (2 stitches each side every 2nd round) so that one decreasing-point is vertically over the center of the thumb. Then the thumb will stick out nicely, and until the mittens are worn, R and L will be identical. After the first few dozen snowballs are made they will differ unmistakably, and it will take decisive blocking to alter their ways. If you have the kindness and foresight to present them in sets of three, the loss of the first one will not be irremediable.

Very small children's mittens may be attached to each other by a knitted or crocheted cord passed through the sleeve of the winter jacket, then if the mittens are abandoned in a carefree moment, they insist on remaining with the wearer. This cord is rather umbilical, and is one of the first things eliminated by the kindergartner as babyish.

For babies, by the way, I do not fuss with mittens at all. A cord threaded through the edge of the sweater-cuff and firmly tied over the hands keeps them fine and warm. You can attach bells to it if such things divert your baby.

Don't knit mittens too tightly, especially for small children. Tight knitting is rather unyielding and stiff; fairly loose knitting conforms better to the hand and is just as warm. 5 stitches to 1″ in knitting worsted is quite firm enough.

Be sure to make the cuffs generously long; palms *will* shrink up, and this pulls the cuffs shorter and shorter. Recently I have been experimenting with quite large cuffs, intended to enclose the coat- or jacket-cuff. If you mentally compare a long skinny mitten inside a large coat-cuff with a broad-cuffed mitten which encloses the coat-cuff, you may perhaps agree that the latter will block icy blasts more effectively.

I DON'T KNOW WHEN I'VE ENJOYED A SPRING SO MUCH. As the winter was long and hard, so has it been slow in ending, but last week we went to the Kingcup Swamp and dug up a likely-looking clump with many buds. It was put in a soup-tureen with a yellow border, and at first kept outside the front door so that it could get used to being far from home. Then we brought it inside, and today it is blooming brilliantly with flowers of such a blazing yellow that in anything else I would consider the color less than pleasing.

Color (and you may consider this to apply to the choice of wool for mittens) is a deeply subjective matter; in the tastes of various people it can vary infinitely. They say animals can't perceive color—(how *did* they find out?) Colorblind people—what do *they* see? As there are different degrees of color-blindness, may there not be variations in the colors any of us see? If I could see the grass today through someone else's eyes I might suddenly see it as blue. Or greenish-grey. But others may have always seen it as blue or grey, and have learned to call what they see "green", and to describe it as bright, or faded, or rich, or soothing to the eye. Perhaps this accounts for preference in colors. Why do I love red? Why do others love bright violet? Are we really seeing the same color, but describing it differently?

Most people luckily prefer the colors which suit them best, although some blue-eyed ones become heartily sick of blue if they have been largely dressed to match their eyes as children.

Then there is the matter of associations. For years I loathed purple because it was the color of a droopy and voluminous hand-me-down coat I had to wear. Salmon-pink I can't stand perhaps because it used to be the color of so much cheap underwear, but in smoked salmon it's delicious, and it suits geraniums and zinnias. In fact in flowers one tends to like almost any color under the sun.

Experiment with mittens, and exercise and expand your sense of color with them. Combine unusual colors, and find out if you like the result. Use up odds and ends of wool for stripes or patterns.

When making mittens on four needles with color-patterns, cast on a few more stitches then usual, as it may be hard to knit around in patterns and still keep the work loose. A beginner sometimes finds vertical stripes of looseness where he changes from needle to needle. He learns to correct this by working the first stitch on each needle quite tightly. When this habit is carried into a color-pattern mitten or stocking it can result in a tightness in the carried color which is practically unavoidable. Don't worry about it; use more stitches. By the same token, color-patterned mittens should be large. They don't stretch much and nothing is horrider than a tight mitten.

EXPERIMENTATION WITH NORWEGIAN MITTENS can be fascinating, but some planning is necessary. Decide how wide your mitten is to be—50 to 60 stitches is quite usual, but much depends on the wool you are using. Earmark three stitches on either side for vertical stripes running up between the back and the palm. It looks pretty to work the first and third of them in the pattern-color, and the middle one alternately in the two colors. This results in a narrow ladder-like stripe, which you can vary if you wish.

In a 56-stitch mitten you will then have 25 stitches each for palm and back. The palm is usually worked in a small repetitive pattern, which lends itself easily to the infiltration of the thumb-increasing (in this type of mitten the thumb should *not* stick out at the side). I like to start the thumb-shaping right after the wrist. Select two stitches for its beginning—usually the stitches next to the vertical line, or one or two stitches from it—and increase two stitches between them every third round, using M 1 as the increase-method. You may also increase every second or every fourth round. In any case, when 10 stitches have been increased (roughly one-fifth of the total of 56 stitches) work without further shaping until you are at the beginning of the thumb. Perform the Thumb Trick on 10 sts (see p. 145) and work straight up the mitten until you reach the tip of the little finger. I like to decrease then quite fast—four stitches *every* round—until the knitting comes to a point of perhaps 8 stitches, and is fastened off. Make use of the vertical stripes at the sides for decreasing, thus: work to within 1 stitch of vertical line, K 2 together, K 1, SSK.

The cuff-pattern is frequently different from that on the mitten-back, and can contrast to it strongly. For instance, on a mitten with an angular star-snowflake on its back, the cuff may be ornamented with a graceful scroll. The unorthodox mixing of designs heightens the rustic appearance of these charming mittens. I have taken it upon myself to accentuate this characteristic with a special border, which is worked thus:

Idiot-Cord Border:
Work a piece of Idiot-Cord (see Appendix) long enough to go around the mitten-border; that is, it should contain as many rounds as you wish stitches cast on. (If your cuff-pattern contains slightly more stitches than the hand of the mitten, this is all to the good, as it makes the cuff flare out. Decrease, on the palm side, when the cuff is finished.) For the Idiot-cord choose wool of a quite startling color—any color in the world will contrast pleasantly with the cream-and-oatmeal or black-and-white of traditional patterned mittens. Join the beginning of this cord to its end as best you can—even by weaving—being careful not to twist it. Then, with sock-needles and the contrasting color, knit up one stitch in each round of the cord, purl 1 round with the contrasting color, and start the mitten, rejoicing, I hope, in this technique. (I unvented

it about a year ago, and use it for many borders, thus avoiding the rather monotonous ribbing, as well as the staid and ladylike garter-stitch.)

The bulk of pattern-planning is reserved for the back of the mitten—the part that shows. Here you can have a wonderful time with squared paper, pencil, and (naturally) a giant eraser. Mark off a field of squares 25 wide and very roughly 50 high, and start fitting a pattern—any pattern—into it. Most patterns are on an uneven number of stitches, with the odd stitch as its center-line. This simplifies designing, and the two sides can be mirror-images of each other, so that you actually have to put down only one complete side. Start off with the main motif, be it a star, a stag, crossed skis, or a geometric form such as a circle or diamond. Once you have placed it, interrupt horizontal lines of more than five stitches of one color, so that the wool won't have to be carried too far. Large spaces may be filled with any small design or curlicue that you wish, or even with occasional single stitches.

The tapered end of the mitten may be a continuation of the main pattern or a little taradiddle by itself. Sometimes a bit of judicious cheating is permitted. It concerns nobody but yourself if you carry the wool for more than five stitches and have to twist the threads at the back of the work to prevent long loops; you are not writing this down for posterity; suit yourself. But don't say I told you to, as it complicates instructions, if you are ever called upon to write any. It also makes the project more involved for the novice. It is great fun to stick closely to the conventions of color-pattern knitting, and it renders designing more challenging.

Much of the above applies also to the knitting of Norwegian stockings for cross-country ski-ing. The welcome arrival of this sport in the U.S. will enable you to knit outstanding Christmas presents for any addict, M or F.

TODAY, I TOOK MY KNITTING DOWN TO THE RIVER, as it is time to fish for walleyes. We have 40 acres of slough and woodland, pretty accurately bisected by the Yellow River, which widens slightly at this point, to make a good fishing hole. When we bought the place we thought "Hey! our own fishing hole!" and rubbed our hands together. We soon found that it was everyone else's fishing hole as well, and that they had been coming here, man and boy, for generations. Now things have changed. We're here permanently, and long for privacy. Both our neighbors have posted their land, and ours would have been an inconsistency. Most fortuitously, a fine lake has been dammed up, and stocked with fish, by the Department, just a few miles upstream (and has incidentally played old hob with our regular fish-population). Here people can park, fish, picnic, and whoop it up to their hearts' content, smiled upon benignly by the State.

We posted. Two "NO TRESPASSING" signs, two lengths of stout wire, one handpainted sign saying ᴎO FɪꙄHɪᴎɡ at the base of which we put an indicting pile of used cans , and the deed was done. We felt awful, and sat back to wait for Unpleasantness.

We were most agreeably surprised. People are sensitive; they are accommodating. Not one has expostulated. Some say they wonder why we held out so long before posting. The strongest thing they say is, "I guess a few guys spoiled it, didn't they?" I guess they are right. We value our peace and quiet excessively, and the attitude of the good guys has removed all pangs of guilt, greed, and selfishness.

It is with difficulty that we resist the impulse to put up a sign saying PLEAꙄE FɪꙄH But no; it is too pleasant to sit alone on the edge of one's own river bank to fish and unvent revolutionary mittens.

I don't remember what got me started in the first place unless it was the decision to approach the mitten from a new angle. I decided to ginger it up with some mitering. The technique of the miter is the practice of that old favorite, the zigzag afghan pattern. If you regularly decrease at some points and increase at the same number of points, and alternate these two shapings, your work will zigzag up and down but keep the same number of stitches. *De*creasing two stitches cause the zig to go down, *in*creasing two stitches causes the zag to go up.

If I constructed the whole mitten on the miter principle, and used four miters, two pointing up and two pointing down so that they neutralized each other, the down-pointing ones could be placed at the back and front of the mitten and would look rather graceful. And who knows what could be done with miters when the time comes to decrease for the top?

Using wool which knits up at about $4\frac{1}{2}$ stitches to $1''$, I cast on 48 stitches, or one-third more than I would for a straight 36-stitch mitten. This was because miters, by their very construction, "take up". I ribbed in K 1, P 1, for five rounds, but you could just as easily start with an Idiot-Cord border, as on the patterned mittens.

The 48 stitches were put on four needles, and a fifth one was used for knitting, because a 4-miter mitten falls neatly into four equal sections. The miters were started right away—2 decreasing ones at front and back and 2 increasing ones at the sides. In order to make things easy for myself I placed half a miter at each end of each of the four needles. Thus on the first needle I increased after the first stitch and knitted the last two stitches together. On the second needle I worked SSK at the beginning, and increased one stitch before the last stitch. This was repeated on the two remaining needles.

Every second round was worked without shaping.

It zigzagged beautifully.

Concerning the thumb I was in a quandary. Might not the queer angle of the knitted rows interfere with its organic position? I hopefully performed the Thumb-Trick (see Appendix) at 45° and knitted on, quite willing to rip if necessary. A pleasant surprise was in store. After I had picked up the stitches and finished the thumb, it turned out to be just what the doctor ordered—a pleasant anatomical thumb which folded itself docilely across the palm in a positively human fashion.

Cheered, I continued to the top-shaping. This was so simple that I can't believe it has not been attempted before. I just eliminated the increasings at the sides and continued with the front- and back-decreasings until 8 stitches remained. Because I am conscientious, and enjoy being it, I wove back and front together, but you could just as easily run the wool through the stitches and fasten off.

This was the very first mitered mitten. Since then I have never bothered to plan ahead with the Thumb-Trick. I complete the mitten, sans thumb, try it on, and snip just one stitch at the joint of the thumb at the center of the panel. I then unravel in both directions until 15 stitches are exposed, and complete the thumb on them (see Afterthought Pocket, p. 146).

If you want to be devious, there is a way of shaping the cuff, if this mitten is too straight for you. Start with 4, or perhaps 8, stitches too many. When

you arrive at the wrist, omit the increases on one or two rounds. This will
nip in the wrist. You may also make a short string or piece of Idiot-Cord,
take a hitch in the back with it, and tie it in a knot or bow.

Need I say that this is a godgiven mitten for those who save their scraps
of wool?

Norwegian Mitten Graph

PITHY DIRECTIONS: NORWEGIAN MITTENS 12″ LONG, 9″ AROUND HAND.

They should be large.

GAUGE: 6 sts to 1″

MATERIALS: 4 oz ea. 2-ply Sheepswool in Main Color and Contrasting Color. Or any wool to give correct GAUGE. 1 set 9″ sock-needles of a size to give *you* correct GAUGE. *Cast on* 54 sts and rib 5 rnds, or make Idiot-Cord border as in text. K 3 rnds MC and put in cuff-pattern. K 3 rnds MC, then K 1 rnd, P 1 rnd CC. K 3 rnds MC, decreasing to 46 sts by K 2 tog 8 times across front. K 1 rnd CC, 1 rnd alternate colors, 1 rnd CC. Start patterns, having large one on back, small one repeated on palm, and 3 neutral sts running up sides. Immediately mark 2 sts for thumb at one side of palm, and inc 2 sts between them every 3rd rnd. When 10 sts have been increased, work straight to thumb at 3″ from wrist. Perform Thumb-Trick on 10 sts (see p. 145). Work straight for 4″ to end of little finger. Decr 1 st each side of 3 neutral sts *every* rnd until 8 or 4 sts remain. Fasten off. Work thumb on 20 sts for 15 rnds. Pull wool through all sts and fasten off.

MITERED MITTENS.
SIZE, AVERAGE ADULT, 8″ AROUND HAND

GAUGE: $4\frac{1}{2}$ sts to 1″.

MATERIALS: 1 4 oz skein 3-ply Sheepswool, or any wool to give correct GAUGE. 1 set of 5 needles to give *you* correct GAUGE.

CAST ON 48 sts. Join, and rib for 5 rnds, or make Idiot-Cord border. Place 12 sts on each of 4 needles, and work with the fifth one. Start Miters:

1st needle: K 1, M 1, K to last 2 sts, K 2 tog.

2nd needle: SSK, K to last st, M 1, K 1.

3rd and 4th needles: Rep 1st and 2nd needles. K 1 rnd. Rep from *. Continue thus until length is sufficient to reach to little finger, or $9\frac{1}{2}$″. Eliminate the M 1 sts and continue until 8 sts remain. Fasten off. Try on, snip 1 st at joint of thumb, unravel in both directions to release 15 sts, pick them up on 3 needles, work 15 rnds and finish off. Neaten thumb-corners with ravelled wool.

JUNE

Borders.
Small Stuff for Summer Knitting:
Three Hats

I WILL COME OUT FLAT-FOOTED and personally disapprove of crocheted borders on knitted cardigans, but without in any way trying to convert those who crochet borders expertly and with pleasure. May their paths run smooth.

As a non-crocheter—at least, at present, although who knows what the future holds?—I can crochet well enough for all practical purposes. I don't enjoy it, however, and I don't prefer its appearance to that of knitting, though I admit that some crocheted things sometimes look neat and warm and pretty, and of course, at present, very fashionable.

Once I was told that one should not mix the grape and the grain, in that case, knitting and crochet, and I seized upon the aphorism with delight, never to abandon it. There is something about a crocheted border on knitting which offends me (again, purely personally), especially as there are good methods of knitting a border, and keeping the project within the confines of a single skill. You realize that I am being highly inconsistent; I love and admire tweed with knitted borders, and have met elegant tweed borders on leather, and vice versa. I guess I just have this low prejudice against crochet—pure snobbery.

However, many knitters will admit to being not very expert in crocheting, and for them I present the knitted garter-stitch border, with a few tricks to make it look very professional indeed.

First, use a smaller-sized needle than you took for the main body of the sweater, and if this is not available, work as tightly as you can. Knit up the stitches of the border in the right relationship to the rows of the fabric, so that the borders will neither flare nor pull tight. The rule on a stocking-stitch cardigan is two stitches knitted up for every three rows of knitting. Thus you knit up one stitch in each of the first two rows, skip the third, and keep repeating this, except for the neck-front and neck-back, where you knit up the stitches as you find them. For the short pieces of neck-sides, do the best you can, trying to stick to the "two stitches for three rows" principle, and keeping the same number of stitches on either side.

For a garter-stitch border on a garter-stitch jacket, knit up *one* stitch for every *two* rows of fabric; that is, one stitch for every ridge.

Make the border as wide as you wish, depending on your taste in borders, or on how much too narrow you may have made your sweater. Wide borders are a splendid way of concealing errors of judgment committed when computing the width of a project! If you want a narrow border, similar to a crocheted one, cast off right away on the second or third row, but remember that such a slight border will not serve to counteract the natural inward curl of stocking-stitch.

On a plain cardigan you may like to work the border in a series of different colors, always remembering to change colors on the right side of the work. Don't forget to increase at the front neck-corners, and to decrease at the inside corners of a square neck. The rate of increase or decrease is two stitches every second row, one on each side of the corner-stitch. Phyllis likes to keep her corner-stitch in stocking-stitch on the right side, by purling it on the wrong side, and very nice her corners always look. Smart Barbara Walker combines her inside-corner-stitch with its attendant decreases by working sl 2 tog as if to K, K 1, pass 2 sl sts over.

Backs of necks often want to stretch out of shape, and a decreased border is a first-rate way of keeping them in order. Decrease quite suddenly when the border is half-completed. Decide how wide you want the back of your neck by measuring—it is usually around 5″–6″. Then stretch a piece of your project as wide as you conveniently can and count the number of stitches to 5 or 6 inches in the stretched piece. The result is the number of stitches for the edge of the neck-back; decrease down to this number, evenly-spaced across, give or take a stitch. Don't rely on tight casting-off to hold in a neck-back.

Casting off a border is a bit on the tricky side—better to have it too loose than too tight, but better still to have it just right. Keep trying and ruthlessly ripping until you attain this ideal condition. On a garter-stitch border cast off in *purl*, on the *right* side, or use one of my two cast-off methods in the Appendix.

Garter-stitch—although excellent—is not the only stitch for borders. Seed-stitch looks well if firmly worked, and ribbing may also be used if you are careful to center it correctly at the corners. Beware, however, of using any stitch which tends to curl, such as stocking-stitch or reverse-stocking-stitch, unless you wish for this special effect.

Another of my prejudices is against cardigans faced with ribbon. Sometimes the ribbon shrinks in washing; sometimes, alas, the sweater. Ribbon is more stubborn to wash than wool, so you scrub at it, with deleterious results to the knitted fabric. Putting ribbon on a border is an expert's job; one often has to pay to have it done, and, worse, wait for days until it *is* done. Once it is on, it is on for good, machine-made buttonholes and all; it can't be ripped as a knitted border can, and if the job hasn't been done with TLC, there you are; stuck. Besides, although a sweater-border should be firm, it should not have the rigidity of ribbon. A knitted garment is elastic by definition, and no part of it should have the firmness of woven material.

A GOOD SUMMER PROJECT IS A BEVY OF HATS. They don't take much wool, and are an excellent means of using up leftovers and oddments in the form of stripes or color-patterns. They share with socks and mittens the quality of portability, and are an admirable way to get the jump on next winter's weather and the present-giving season. I prefer to make them in the round on a 16″ circular needle, keeping a set of four sock-needles handy for the last few rounds at the top.

Do not feel that you are in any way obliged to possess perfect sets of four needles. Emergency and experiment have taught me that a very motley quartet will finish off a hat quite adequately. I have made a hat on a #$10\frac{1}{2}$ circular needle and finished it on a set of #5s simply because at the moment I could find none larger. Of course I had to work loosely on the #5s, but the thick wool which had necessitated the $\#10\frac{1}{2}$ in the first place made this easy; it was only for a few rounds anyway.

A couple of unmatching needles in a set also present no difficulty to the loose knitter who can adjust GAUGE to the thickness of the wool, rather than to needle-size. Try out your own reactions to such unorthodox tools and conditions; you may surprise and please yourself.

A friend returning from foreign parts once brought me a *Maltese Fisherman's Hat* to copy. It was knitted at $5\frac{1}{2}$ stitches to $2''$ in very thick natural wool, hairier than, but similar to, Sheepsdown, and I had a fine time puzzling out its construction. A wide band of garter-stitch encircled neck-back and ears, which it hugged in a very comforting fashion. The decreasing looked erratic at first, but it turned out to have been worked in a quite logical spiral by purling two stitches together at four points every second round. The shaping I considered rather unsubtle—it did not vary at all towards the top—until I decided that it contributed to the possibly traditional piscatorial shape of the cap, which ends in a rather Mediterranean point, crowned by a ridiculous tassel of a couple of dozen ends. I made them still more antic by cutting them at different lengths and putting a knot at the end of each. But you needn't.

The completed cap is quite similar to the original. My one radical alteration was to shape the back of the neck more anatomically by increasing six stitches quite sharply at this point. If you want to make an exact reproduction, cast on six more stitches to start with, and omit this increasing when you come to it. Maltese Hat directions are at the end of the chapter, along with those for the "Ganomy" (gnome to you) and the Three-Cornered hats.

The *Ganomy Hat* is made of fairly thick wool (4 stitches to $1''$) on the same miter principle which governs the making of mitered mittens in the previous chapter. (Fan-and-Feather stitch is based broadly on the same principle, except that the shaping is more spread out, and you end up with waves instead of zigzags.)

Now, caps rarely cover the ears adequately unless provided with earlaps for this purpose; one is constantly dragging them down over the ears. Let us build two down-pointing miters into the sides of a cap. That means that we shall have to cast on a surprising number of stitches, since mitering consumes them at a great rate, and we don't want our cap to disappear like a blown-out candle-flame before it can even be tried on. Better still, let us supplement the down-pointing miters with an up-pointing mitre at forehead and nape. As we eat up stitches over each ear, so shall we continue to produce them at the same rate on the forehead and at the back of the neck.

To cut a long story fairly short, that is what I am doing, sitting on a sandbank in the river. I cast on 80 stitches with a 16″ needle, made about 1″ of garter-stitch border, and then started shaping, *de*creasing 2 stitches at each side and *in*creasing 2 stitches at front and at back every second round. I have more stitches between the ears and the forehead than I do between the ears and the nape of the neck on account of the anatomy of the human head. About twice as many. How you increase and decrease is up to you—one way is as good as another, depending on your tastes and prejudices—as long as you keep it strictly vertical. At chapter's end you will find a fairly workmanlike method.

Why must a Tam-o'-Shanter be round? Can't it be octagonal, pentagonal, square or triangular? I've not tried out the first three, but I've made a *Three-Cornered Hat,* and it finds favor with all who try it on. Wear it down or up, with the point to the front or the back, or with all points tucked in—it has as many lives as a cat.

Start by casting on sufficient stitches to go comfortably and adequately around the head. Work an inch of border—ribbed or garter-stitch—and then increase to half-as-many-stitches-again by working K 2, M 1, across. (I work garter-stitch borders back-and-forth because I am lazy about purling, and because I don't mind sewing up a short seam. You may make them around in alternate rounds of knit and purl if you wish.) Join, and continue on a 16″ circular needle. Mark two stitches at three equidistant points by putting a smallish safety-pin in the fabric; you can put a ring-marker each side of the pairs of stitches if you wish. Increase 1 stitch each side of the marked stitches every second round—six stitches per increase-round, that is; a rate which keeps things fairly flat. (Eight stitches would make it absolutely flat; remember this when you design a square hat.)

After about $3\frac{1}{2}''$, stop increasing. I give my hat a sharply demarcated line of turn before starting to decrease, and you may like to do the same: purl one round, knit two rounds (or more if you like), purl one round, all without shaping.

Then start *de*creasing at the same places and at the same rate—6 stitches every second round. After $2\frac{1}{2}''$, change to decreasing *every* round, so that the top of the hat will lie flat. When you are down to very few stitches—say 6, or even 3—finish off.

PITHY DIRECTIONS: MALTESE FISHERMAN'S HAT.

GAUGE: $5\frac{1}{2}$ sts to $2''$; 11 sts to $4''$.

MATERIALS: 1 4 oz skein Sheepsdown or thick wool to give above GAUGE. 1 $16''$ circular needle, 1 set large sock-needles, to give *you* above GAUGE.

Cast on 36 sts. K back-and-forth for 10 rows (5 ridges). NOW:

K 17, turn, K back. K 15, turn, K back. K 13, turn, K back.

K 11, turn, K back, K 9, turn, K back. K 7, turn, K back. THEN:

K 8, turn, K back. K 10, turn, K back. K 12, turn, K back.

K 14, turn, K back. K 16, turn, K back. K to end of row. (I like to slip all first sts.) Repeat the foregoing on the other side. *Ear-shaping finished.*

K 1 complete row. Next row: K 15, (M 1, K 1) 6 times, K 15, cast on 14 for front. *Join.* There should and *must* be 56 sts. Work around for 10 rnds of stocking-stitch (more for a deeper hat), keeping the 14 front-sts in garter-st for 2 ridges by purling them on the 1st and 3rd rnds.

SHAPE TOP: Decrease 4 sts evenly-spaced around (P 2 tog, K 12) 4 times. K 1 rnd. Rep these 2 rnds, having 1 st less between decreasings every 2nd rnd. When 8 sts remain, finish off. Make the tassel of your dreams.

GANOMY HAT

GAUGE 4 sts to 1″. 16 sts to 4″.

MATERIALS: 1 4 oz skein of any wool suitable for above GAUGE. 1 16″ needle, 1 set sock-needles suitable for above GAUGE for *you*.

Cast on 80 sts. K back-and-forth for 8 rows (4 ridges). *Join* and work around. Keep marker between last and first sts, for the beginning anyway.

Rnd 1. K 1, M 1, K 11, K 2 tog, SSK, (L ear) K 23, M 1, K 2, M 1, (front) K 23, K 2 tog, SSK, (R ear) K 11, M 1, K 1 (back).

Rnd 2. K around. Rep these 2 rnds to a total of $4\frac{1}{2}$″. Stop front-increasing, but continue with other shapings to total of $6\frac{1}{2}$″ or as high as you want. Stop back-increasing, but continue with side-decreasings until 14 sts remain. K 6 rnds. Finish off.

Bobble: insert pingpong ball (which will cause hat to float in emergency) or a rabble of wool-ends, and wind wool tightly just below it.

THREE-CORNERED HAT

GAUGE: $5\frac{1}{2}$ sts to 2″. 11 sts to 4″.

MATERIALS: 1 4 oz skein Sheepsdown or thick wool to give *you* the above GAUGE. 1 16″ circular needle, 1 set of large sock-needles, to give *you* above GAUGE.

Cast on 36 sts. K back-and-forth for 5 rows ($2\frac{1}{2}$ ridges). Next row: K 2, M 1, across (54 sts). *Join* and knit around. Mark 2 sts at three equidistant points with 16 sts between. *Now:* *K to 2 marked sts, M 1, K 2, M 1. Rep from * twice more. K 1 rnd. Rep these 2 rnds until you have 84 sts. *Stop Increasing.* P 1 rnd. K 2 rnds. P 1 rnd.

Start decreasing: *K to within 1 st of marked sts, K 2 tog, SSK. Rep from * twice more. K 1 rnd. Rep these 2 rnds until you have 48 sts. Now decr. *every* rnd until you have 6 sts. Finish off.

JULY

A Shawl: Good Travel-Knitting.
Bonus: One Row Buttonhole

JULY IS TRAVEL-MONTH.

Aged couples such as we pay no heed. We do not wish to become part of traffic, let alone a statistic. We sit snug in our snug yard, letting travel mean nothing more to us than a faint swish from the main road—swish of families heading inexorably north, satisfied and exhausted south. We shall hold our fire until later, when crowds thin and the mosquito retreats.

When you set out on the annual family trip naturally you have to take your knitting; *something* has to keep you sane in face of the possibly quite ferocious situations you will be up against in the next two weeks.

Try a shawl.

Do not scoff; it is perfect travel-knitting, as I have proved to myself many times. A round shawl, in fine wool, on a circular needle, is my invariable companion when space is limited, waiting-around probable, and events uncertain.

First of all, fine wool takes up little space, but affords plenty of actual knitting.

Secondly, a circular needle can hardly get lost unless you pull it out by main force and cast it from you. The worst that can happen is the escape (soon remedied) of a few stitches.

You are now practically suffocating by holding your breath in order to burst out and say, "But a shawl is *difficult*".

71

My dears, it's not. I have a circular shawl for you which starts at the center, has absolutely no pattern, and only six shaping-rounds in the whole thing. These shaping-rounds occur farther and farther apart, when there are (because of previous shaping-rounds) a larger and larger number of stitches. Towards the end, by the time your state of mind has become more and more frayed, and your need of mindless comfort greater and greater, your knitting will be nothing but almost endless rounds of hundreds of stitches, with no thinking required, at all. You will end up with an heirloom. Pay attention, therefore. . . .

Need it be said that the first and most important step is to choose the best material available? I, of course, use wool; if you are unluckily sensitive to this lovely stuff, go to a really good wool shop and take the suggestion of the sales clerk. Buy plenty, making an arrangement as to the return of unused skeins, if accompanied by their sales-slip.

Don't necessarily stick to white, or even to pastel colors. One of the loveliest shawls I know is deep barn-red, and another is in alternating and ever-widening circles of two shades of oatmeal. Grey cannot be beat. Use your instinct, even should it tell you that navy, or a mild and gentle green, or deep brown or black would go with all your clothes and suit you best.

Choose two circular needles of a size to knit the wool at a very loose GAUGE— that is to say, a much larger GAUGE than usual. GAUGE, for once in your life, is unimportant, except that it be loose. A 16″ needle is for starters; a 24″ one for everything else. You will find that, unless you wish, a 27″, 30″, 36″ and 48″ needle are not necessary. A 24″ needle will easily handle up to 1000 stitches in fine wool loosely worked. For the very beginning, until you have about 50 stitches, you will have to struggle with four needles, but it's all in a day's work, and soon over.

All set now? Go into a quiet corner for the first few rounds, with an implement I forgot to mention—a crochet-hook—and make Emily Ocker's circular beginning with nine stitches (see Appendix).

Knit one round. If you are unfamiliar with 4-needle knitting, consult the nearest knitting manual; this 4-needle stage won't last long. Don't let your awkwardness worry you, or the sliding about of needles; you are their boss, and they know it.

On the second round double the number of stitches by working Yarn Over, Knit 1, three times on each of the three needles—18 stitches.

Knit 3 rounds plain. Put a safety-pin in the knitted fabric at the beginning of the round to help you remember which is the first needle. Work a second increase-round of YO, K 1, six times on each needle—36 stitches.

Knit 6 rnds. plain. Work a third increase-round—72 stitches (16″ needle)

Knit 12 rnds. plain. Work a fourth increase-round—144 stitches.

Knit 24 rnds. plain. Work a fifth increase-round—288 stitches.

Knit 48 rnds. plain. Work a sixth increase-round—576 stitches.

Knit 96 rounds plain? Well, not really. Before you have knitted half-way to 96 you will be enjoying the strong impression that your shawl is large enough, and you may well be at home again.

Have you begun to see the well-known geometric theory behind what you have been doing? If you are a man, you will have spotted it right away. If you are a woman (sorry, lib), you probably expunged such theories from your memory the minute you finished high school, or even college, to make room for more useful stuff. It's Pi; the geometry of the circle hinging on the mysterious relationship of the circumference of a circle to its radius. A circle will double its circumference in infinitely themselves-doubling distances, or, in knitters' terms, the distance between the increase-rounds, in which you double the number of stitches, goes 3, 6, 12, 24, 48, 96 rounds, and so on to 192, 394, 788, 1576 rounds for all I know. Theory is theory, and I have no intention of putting it into practice, as I do not plan to make a lace carpet for a football field.

When you have worked 40–50 rounds on 576 stitches, you will have created a stunning circular shawl roughly 72″ across—large enough for anybody. Finish it off, probably wash it, and block it on the largest bed in the house, or on a well-vacuumed rug, stretching it severely, and keeping it stretched until dry with dozens, scores, even hundreds of pins stuck into the mattress or rug.

Finish it off, you are saying, how?

There are two ways. The first one is good. Hunt up that crochet-hook, put it in the last stitch you knitted and *chain 6. Now put it through the next three stitches and join them with a slip-stitch. Repeat from *, and continue thus around. You finish off the knitted stitches and form a series of chained loops all at once. Make the loops as long as you wish, and gather more of the knitted stitches together in those slip-stitches if your taste dictates. I no longer finish shawls in this fashion, so have not much of an opinion to offer. When you block an edge of this kind, stick one pin through each chained loop, pulling it out firmly, and the result will be a dainty lacy border. You can pin out every second loop, or every third. To repeat myself—experiment.

The second method of edging a shawl is one I can't imagine that I alone unvented, but I certainly discovered it in my own brain single-handed. It consists of knitting on a border, but sideways. You *could* knit a very long strip and sew it on, but the sewing-stitches might easily pop when the shawl was stretched. Also to cast off the final round of the shawl loosely enough in the first place is tantamount to impossible. Do, instead, this:

When the shawl is big enough, suddenly, at the beginning of the round, cast on eight stitches by knitting them on in the old-fashioned way. (I tell you, there is *nothing* in knitting which is not useful on occasion.) Knit seven of these stitches, and knit the eighth together with its neighbor-stitch on the last row of the shawl. *Turn, knit 8. Turn, knit 7, knit 2 together. Repeat from *. (See Appendix).

You will think at first that this is going to be an infinite job, but press on, and after a few inches you will find that it is well worth the effort. You are making an elegantly simple but solid border of garter-stitch which will wear excellently, and which will not curl up. You may make it wider if you wish, but not much narrower, or it will be ineffective. You may employ one of Grandma's lace edgings, especially if the shawl is a plain one. You may mark your progress by a row of holes (yarn over, knit 2 together) every so often, or even by single holes. You may increase and subsequently decrease along the outer edge to make points, waves, or scallops. You may put the private stamp of your individuality on your shawl by doing none of these, but something you have just unvented.

Do you mind the word "unvented"? I like it. *In*vented sounds to me rather pompous and conceited. I picture myself as a knitting inventor, in a clean white coat, sitting in a workshop full of tomes of reference, with charts and graphs on the walls. Not real knitters' charts, which are usually scribbled on odd and dog-eared pieces of squared paper, or even ordinary paper with homemade squares on it, but charts like sales charts, and graphs like the economy. I have a thoughtful expression behind my rimless glasses and hold a neatly-sharpened pencil. Who knows but that I don't have a bevy of hand-knitters in the backroom, tirelessly toiling at the actual knit and purl of my deathless designs?

Rubbish.

But *un*vented—ahh! One un-vents something; one unearths it; one digs it up, one runs it down in whatever recesses of the eternal consciousness it has gone to ground. I very much doubt if *any*thing is really new when one works in the prehistoric medium of wool with needles. The products of science and technology may be new, and some of them are quite horrid, but *knitting?* In knitting there are ancient possibilities; the earth is enriched with the dust of the millions of knitters who have held wool and needles since the beginning of sheep. Seamless sweaters and one-row buttonholes; knitted hems and phoney seams—it is unthinkable that these have, in mankind's history, remained undiscovered and unknitted. One likes to believe that there is memory in the fingers; memory undeveloped, but still alive.

I have known of two instances of this in my experience with wool.

Many years ago I was provided with genuine Irish instructions, and permitted to make the first Aran sweater I had ever seen or heard of, for *Vogue Pattern Book*. For this purpose I took unbleached wool and needles with me the next time we went weekend-camping. Those were the palmy days of camping, when firewood and campsites were plentiful, and the ranks of the faithful so uncluttered that one was not eternally threading one's way between neighbors' washlines and campfire smoke. We arrived at the Mississippi, set up camp, and took to the water, me, of course, with my knitting. All day long, in perfect early-summer weather, we were dandled by the milky ripples of the young but already mighty Miss. I puzzled over the directions, which included no picture of what I was actually making, the unaccustomed terms of back twist and forward twist made themselves gradually at home in my brain, the oiled wool slipped through my fingers, ". . . the sun beat down upon it all, and thus my dream began". Not quite a dream, but a strong feeling that my fingers knew quite well what they were about, and welcomed the chance to be about it again after a long lapse of time. I knew then that I had been through this before, with younger fingers in a ruder boat, rocked on the salty summer waves of the Atlantic off the Irish coast. Silly? No.

The second time was with my wheel. A few years ago Christmas was enriched for me by the magnificent gift of an elegant handmade spinning-wheel. Hand-spinning was a skill which I have always regarded with as much awe as those of making bread, and performing the mysterious rite of proper mayonnaise. I have mastered the last two, but I danced and dodged hopefully around my wheel for nearly a year, starting and stopping, trying to understand how it worked, and how it could twist the fibers and wind them on the spindle at the same time. This has often been explained to me, and I still don't understand it.

Since I knew no spinners, the technique of the actual spinning had to be gleaned from a couple of excellent books, but to this day I spin in an ivory tower; I am entirely self-taught, and until recently had never seen anyone else spinning. My fingers, however, were more encouraged than not by the isolation. Now, when I set the treadle in motion, they take on a life of their own. My spinning may be unorthodox, but my fingers know exactly what they are doing, and lumpy but real knitting-wool results. When the fed fibers threaten to become suddenly too thin, my left thumb and forefinger give them a quick extra twist to keep them together until they are safely on the spindle. Why is this? I certainly never cogitated on the matter; my fingers doped it out for themselves. I can only think that centuries of genes have given fingers inherited skills of which we wot not. I know that spinning sets me in a trance; it soothes me and charges my batteries at the same time. When times are tough I sit down to spin during the news-broadcasts, with therapeutic results.

Knitting, as you well know, is therapy too. Why else did you take that shawl on vacation?

One of my early shawls went with me on an air-trip to Spain, and proved invaluable. I had started it at home, and brought it as far as the 16″ needle stage. Soon, at 144 stitches and Lisbon airport, it was on the 24″ needle, and it zigzagged about Europe with me for two or three weeks before returning home, completed. On its circular needle it formed its own knitting-bag to contain the ball of wool. When I was through knitting for a while, I tied the two needle-ends into half a knot and stuffed the whole business into my traveling bag. Even when the shawl was quite large I could get it in easily, so fine was the beautiful Shetland wool I was using.

You might think that a trip of this kind leaves no time for knitting, but you are misled. Sometimes all the new impressions and excitement prove just too much for the uprooted homebody, and she needs to unwind, and return to normal for a shorter or a longer space.

It was a business trip for the Old Man, and you know how that goes: "Dear, I don't know when I'll be done today. Wait for me in the hotel from tea time on". How agonizing to Wait In The Hotel with all Seville or Interlaken or Munich without, imploring to be wandered in. Knitting makes these trying periods easier. Then think of the necessary hanging about in airports. Imagine how good it feels to sit on a foreign park-bench, unpack wool and needle, and pretend you are one of the townswomen, observing the pranks and capers of the tourists. Knitting is for the traveller—there's no doubt of this in my mind—and let us pity the ignorance of the non-knitter and despise her, as would Fanny Squeers, except that no True Knitter would be guilty of despising anybody.

If you are at home, with knitting-books and pattern-books at your elbow, you may insert any lace-pattern you please between the increasing-rounds of your shawl, or you can put in imitation increase-rounds between the real ones at regular intervals by working Yarn Over, K 2 together, instead of Yarn Over, Knit 1. Put them in every sixth round, and they will fit perfectly between the increase-rounds.

You may care to finish off a plain shawl with five or six inches of a pattern-stitch, and then a plain sideways border. I gaze at one as I write. It is loosely made, at a large GAUGE (about 3 stitches to 1″) in pale blue 2-ply Finnish wool. Right after the last increase, when I had 576 stitches, I changed to the

prettiest of patterns, Gull-pattern, which you will find at the end of Chapter
2. After about 2″ of pattern I changed to a deeper blue wool for 2″, then
to a deeper blue yet, then to very dark blue, and then to almost black. After
1″ of almost black I put in an 8-stitch sideways border of garter-stitch with
a semi-Idiot-Cord border (Idiot-Cord every second ridge). See Appendix.

You could also embellish the border with faggotting.

To make faggotting, work Yarn Over, Knit 2 together every row at the same
spot. It will come out differently, depending on where you work it and on
how many stitches you have, but it is always elegant. Try out the following
variations on 8 stitches:

1. K 3, Yarn Over, K 2 together, K to end. Repeat back-and-forth indefinitely.
2. K 4, Yarn Over, K 2 together, K to end. Repeat back-and-forth indefinitely.
3. K 5, Yarn Over, K 2 together, K to end. Repeat back-and-forth indefinitely.

Now add one more stitch (9 stitches) and try out the same three variations.
Isn't it surprising what a difference one stitch can make? Even variations #2
and #5 are subtly different. You will probably have a hard time picking out
which of the six to use.

There is nothing to stop you beginning to shade the colors much sooner,
or using many more of them. Don't forget, when buying wool, that the later
rounds will use up infinitely more wool than the early ones.

Talking of travels and experiments, the following took place in Belgium
a couple of years ago. It was high summer, and we were in Mons for a month.
The Old Man was working, and I had all day to myself. Right after breakfast
in our elegant suite in a rather flossy hotel I would thriftily and thickly butter
the remaining breakfast rolls, pack them in my knitting-bag, and take off, to
wander up and down, down and up, through the steep twisting streets (the
word *Mons* is Latin for mountain), sauntering through the so foreign
supermarkets, sitting in the parks, and returning only in the evening. Museums
were small and dusty, or closed for the summer, and the regular stores didn't
attract me. Belgium, like so much of Europe, has become plasticized, and I'm
not a loot-gatherer at the best of times. The knit-shops had little pure wool,

and the knitting designs, though very fashionable, French, and charming, contained not much that was new in the way of techniques.

I wasn't tempted by the cafés, as I never feel at ease alone in them. I feel conspicuous, although lord knows I'm probably not, and I always imagine that the waiters despise me, which I'm sure they don't have time to do. With the Old Man, I can sit there by the hour, guzzling this and that, and passing snide remarks on everything in sight. It's probably judgment on me when I imagine that others do this to me when I'm alone. Anyway, alone I am miserable in cafés; I always want to be knitting, but don't dare, and usually end up by reading, which makes me good and conspicuous. Therefore no cafés—parks.

Parks are full of single sitters. There is plenty to watch, the green things and the agreeable plantings are a pleasure, and it's nice to be out. I always imagined Belgium to be cowering under incessant downpours of rain most of the time, but that summer (as is so often the case) was most unusual.

A Montois park called Vauxhall was, then, a perfect spot to come to grips with the One-Row Buttonhole. I had heard of one-row buttonholes from all directions; you make it all in one row, they said, and don't have to worry about it on the next row or the row after. Worry? It's a pleasure to spend three rows on a buttonhole. If you are involved in a technical manoeuver, it makes the knitting go like the wind. I was quite content with my own 3-row buttonhole, and not about to confuse myself with improvements.

However, I benevolently tried all the one-row buttonholes as they came along, and found them very ingenious, but truthfully and immodestly, no better-looking then mine. You had to work them back-and-forth, and this entailed turning your knitting twice for each buttonhole, which I, in my laziness, like to avoid.

Here, in Vauxhall Park, I tried them all again. The man at the other end of the bench must have thought I was out of my fur, making buttonhole after buttonhole on a long skinny strip of knitting. I tried combining them, one with another, taking the best parts of each. Lastly I modified them with ideas of my own—all manner of castings-off, of castings-on, of neatenings of corners.

There must have been over thirty buttonholes on my long strip. The favorite was written down in my little black book, and this is what it says:

Mons. August '70.
Definitive (I think) Buttonhole. One Row. 3 stitches.
Slip 1 stitch as if to purl.
Wool Forward and *leave it there.* Slip 1 as if to purl.
Pass first slipped stitch over second. Slip 1 as if to purl.
Pass second slipped stitch over third. Slip 1 as if to purl.
Pass third slipped stitch over fourth.
Put fourth stitch on lefthand needle, reversing it.
Reverse, twist, or turn last stitch on righthand needle.
Pull wool tightly, lay it over righthand needle from front to back and pass the turned stitch over it. Make four *firm* backward loops over righthand needle, knit two together. KNIT ON.

There. And I don't even have to turn my work. Other versions have to be turned because they all employ some form of knitting-on the stitches; sometimes four, sometimes three. I much prefer the backward loop in a case like this. If firmly made, it is neat and unobtrusive.

(Backward loop casting-on is of little use at the beginning of a project; there it is nearly always too tight, and hard to work into without unsightly gaps. If you think of it objectively, the regular long-tail method of casting on is based on this method, but you are working the backward-loop-casting-on and the first knitted row simultaneously. Now don't laugh at me; go into a room by yourself, give your mind to it, and see if I'm not right.)

There is one amendment in the little black book; it says, "Work into the back of the cast-on stitches when working garter-stitch; in stocking-stitch, don't." This naturally applies to 2-needle knitting, back-and-forth. I can think of few occasions when one would make buttonholes in circular knitting, so shall not even bother to experiment.

PITHY DIRECTIONS: PLAIN SHAWL, CIRCULAR, ABOUT 72" ACROSS.

GAUGE: about 3 sts to 1"

MATERIALS: 3–4 4oz wheels single-ply Icelandic wool. 10–12 oz Shetland wool, or approximate amount of any yarn which works up at above GAUGE. 1 set sock-needles, 1 16", 1 24" circular needle of a size to give above GAUGE. Approx. #7–#10½.

Cast on 9 by Emily Ocker's method (see Appendix). Place on 3 needles and K 1 rnd.

Next rnd: *Yarn Over, K 1. Rep from * around. (18 sts)
K 3 rnds.

Next rnd: *Yarn Over, K 1. Rep from * around. (36 sts)
K 6 rnds.

Next rnd: *Yarn Over, K 1. Rep from * around. (72 sts)
K 12 rnds.

Next rnd: *Yarn Over, K 1. Rep from * around. (144 sts)
K 24 rnds.

Next rnd: *Yarn Over, K 1. Rep from * around. (288 sts)
K 48 rnds.

Next rnd: *Yarn Over, K 1. Rep from * around. (576 sts)
K about 40 rnds or until tired.

BORDER: "Knit on" 8 sts. *K 7, K 2 tog (the 8th st plus 1 st of shawl). Turn, K 8. Turn. Rep from * until you have knitted off all the last rnd of stitches. Join end of border to beginning.

SHAWL WITH CONCENTRIC CIRCLES OF HOLES.

As above, except that you work a round of Yarn over, K 2 tog every 6th rnd between the increases.

Lace-Pattern for Border:

(This is *Loop Edging* from "A Second Treasury of Knitting Patterns" by Barbara Walker. There are 45 other lace edgings in this book—all lovely.)

Cast on 11 sts.
Row 1. K 3, (YO, SSK, K 1) twice, (YO) twice, K 1, (YO) twice, K 1.
Row 2. (K 2, P 1) 4 times, K 3. (On this row each double YO is treated as
   2 sts, the first being knitted, the second purled.)
Row 3. K 3, YO, SSK, K 1, YO, SSK, K 7.
Row 4. Bind off 4 sts, K 3, P 1, K 2, P 1, K 3.
Rep rows 1–4.

Three Lace-Patterns for Shawl:

   I. When there are 144 sts, K 3 rnds.
Rnd 1.   K 5, *YO, K 2 tog, K 10. Rep from * around, ending K 5, place
           marker. Be sure you have exactly 144 sts, and begin and end rnds
           with odd sts as indicated, or your pattern will be off.
Rnd 2. and all even-numbered rnds, K.
Rnd 3.   K 3, *SSK, YO, K 1, YO, K 2 tog, K 7. Rep from * around, ending
           K 4.
Rnd 5.   K 2, *SSK, YO, K 3, YO, K 2 tog, K 5. Rep from * around, ending
           K 3.
Rnd 7.   K 1, *SSK, YO, K 5, YO, K 2 tog, K 3. Rep from * around, ending
           K 2.
Rnd 9.   *SSK, YO, K 7, YO, K 2 tog, K 1. Rep from * around.
Rnd 11. K 2, *YO, K 2 tog, K 3, SSK, YO, K 5. Rep from *, ending K 3.
Rnd 13. K 3, *YO, K 2 tog, K 1, SSK, YO, K 7. Rep from *, ending K 4.
Rnd 15. K 4, *YO, sl 1, K 2 tog, pass slipped st over, YO, K 9. Rep from
           * ending K 5.
Rnd 17. K 5, *YO, K 2 tog, K 10. Rep from * around, ending K 5. K 4 rnds.

II. When there are 288 sts K 4 rnds, and rep rnds 1–10 of pattern I.

Rnd 11. *K 2, YO, K 2 tog, K 3, SSK, YO, K 2, SSK, YO, K 9, YO, K 2 tog. Rep from * around.

Rnd 13. K 3, *YO, K 2 tog, K 1, SSK, YO, K 2, SSK, YO, K 11, YO, K 2 tog, K 2, Rep from * around, ending YO, K 2 tog. *Move marker 1 st to left.*

Rnd 15. K 3, *YO, sl 1, K 2 tog, psso, YO, K 2, SSK, YO, K 13, YO, K 2 tog, K 2. Rep from * ending YO, K 2 tog. *Move marker 1 st to left.*

Rnd 17. K 1, *K 2, YO, K 2 tog, K 1, SSK, YO, K 7, YO, K 2 tog, K 6, YO, K 2 tog. Rep from * around. *Move marker 1 st to left.*

Rnd 19. K 4, *SSK, YO, K 6, SSK, YO, K 1, YO, K 2 tog, K 6, YO, K 2 tog, K 3. Rep from * ending YO, K 2 tog. *Move marker 1 st to left.*

Rnd 21. K 2, *SSK, YO, K 6, SSK, YO, K 3, YO, K 2 tog, K 6, YO, K 2 tog, K 1. Rep from * ending YO, K 2 tog. *Move marker 1 st to left.*

Rnd 23. SSK, *YO, K 6, SSK, YO, K 5, YO, K 2 tog, K 6, YO, sl 1, K 2 tog, psso. Rep from *, ending YO, SSK. *Move marker 1 st to left.*

Rnd 25. K 6, *SSK, YO, K 7, YO, K 2 tog, K 6, YO, K 2 tog. K 5. Rep from *, ending YO, K 2 tog. *Move marker 1 st to left.*

Rnd 27. K 4, *SSK, YO, K 9, YO, K 2 tog, K 11. Rep from *, ending K 7.

Rnd 29. K 3, *SSK, YO, K 11, YO, K 2 tog, K 9. Rep from *, ending K 6.

Rnd 31. K 2, *SSK, YO, K 13, YO, K 2 tog, K 7. Rep from *, ending K 5.

Rnd 33. K 1, *SSK, YO, K 15, YO, K 2 tog, K 5. Rep from *, ending K 4.

Rnd 35. *SSK, YO, K 17, YO, K 2 tog, K 3. Rep from *. *Put marker back 1 st.*

Rnd 37. *SSK, YO, K 19, YO, K 2 tog, K 1. Rep from *. *Put marker back 1 st.*

Rnd 39. SSK, *YO, K 21, YO, sl 1, K 2 tog, psso. Rep from *, ending YO, K 2 tog. *Put marker back 1 st.*

Rnd 41. K 1, *YO, K 2 tog, K 22. Rep from *. K 4 rnds.

III. When there are 576 sts, put marker back 6 sts, K 3 rnds. Repeat pattern I. *Move marker forward 6 sts.* Re-repeat pattern I. K 4 rnds. Do not cast off. For plain border, see p. 74.

AUGUST

Christmas Fiddle-Faddle in the Wilds

THIS CHAPTER will be a curiosity of literature.

Exceedingly few old women of over sixty go water-camping in the Canadian north woods. Some of them write picture-postcards, some write home, but I'll bet that not one in a thousand tries to write part of a book. The experienced sympathy of one who has gone through the same travail is something, then, that I shall probably never receive.

I will try to explain.

When the weather is foul one cannot write because all waking hours are used up trying to keep warm, dry, and fed. When the weather is perfect—there is little mixed weather—one must naturally take advantage of it by going on extended trips in the canoe.

In a travelling canoe one cannot write.

Exploration up creeks, over beaver dams, and through mossy but tangled forests takes up more of a writer's time. As soon as the poor but determined creature sits itself down on a boat-cushion against a convenient rock, grabs note-book and pen ostentatiously, assumes an absorbed scowl, and writes just *one* sentence, gentle questions come wafting over the cool sunny air:

Wouldn't you feel more comfortable with your boots off? Do you remember if we brought the soap? Where did we put the soap? Do you remember if I remembered to bring my fish-mouth-holder-opener? Shall we move on somewhere else? And of course that hardy perennial: Isn't it time for a little something to eat?

Accordingly, this chapter will be written in fits and starts, separated by horizontal lines. But it really *is* written in the solitary lands and forests, and the knitted things described really were designed right here, far from telephone, reference library, old scruffy notebooks, wool supplies, and the daily mail. On, then, on. . .

Today was so perfect that we set out after breakfast for an hour and didn't return until suppertime. Fishing went on continuously, so no writing was done, but two small artifacts were achieved in line with the title of this chapter—sheer fiddle-faddle.

If one will employ time and wool to knit doorknob sweaters and cosies for extra rolls of johnpaper, why not include knitted Christmas-tree ornaments? Today I made a star and a tree on two needles. Both are based on the principle that knitting will hump itself up when it is consistently decreased at the same spot.

For the star I decreased two stitches every row at five points until I was down to five stitches. This took no time at all. I had cast on 55 stitches so mine was a very small star of only five rows, which blocked out to $2\frac{1}{2}''$ across. You could cast on 65, 75, 85, to make the star bigger and bigger. Divide the stitches into five equal sections, and place half a section at each end. See end of chapter.

Should you prefer a six-pointed star, cast on six times any uneven number, and decrease at six points instead of five.

Change colors if and when the spirit moves you.

The making of those points set me thinking about the shape of fir-trees. The points in this case must not be so sharp, or the tree would be stunted and frilly: I will decrease every second row instead of every row, and make more points—seven instead of five—one for the top of the tree and three for each side.

OK, then. I cast on 77 stitches (7 × 11) and worked in garter-stitch. Every second row I made seven double-decreases, with eight stitches between them on the first row and four at each end. By the time I was down to 35 stitches (roughly half the original number cast on), I worked to the middle, held the needles like two sides of a skinny triangle, and the seven points started looking like the outline of a tree. To fill the center I worked some short rows on half the stitches, three stitches less each time, and repeated this on the other side, making a short 4-stitch trunk in the process. Then the two halves were woven together. (For garter-stitch weaving, see Appendix).

LAST NIGHT, the moon—three-quarters full—reflected herself in the water behind the triple twisted cedar as in a Japanese print. This morning the print has changed; all the further shores have disappeared, the sun is seen only as a pale radiance, and sky and water have merged and mingled. Tall rushes next to the fireplace mirror themselves unwaveringly in the glassy lake, making one perfect circle, some pointed eggs, and some funny triangles. Slowly, to the scent of coffee, the radiance turns to a silver sun doubled by its own reflection, and the opposite shore appears through the haze. Clearly, another perfect day is coming up.

We packed ourselves into the canoe and set off for a different arm of the lake. I took four #2 needles and some rather fine bluish roving-yarn, and started on the knitted Christmas-angel which has been occupying my mind for the last few days. As always when I start a new design, the moment I cast on the ideas came thick and fast; some of them good, some of them negligible. Things I work out in theory—let alone without a pencil—usually turn out to be lemons; I can design only by doing. This is what I did:

I cast on 56 stitches, because this angel will be started at the bottom of its skirt, with seven ribs of seven stitches and one purled stitch between each: 7 times 8 = 56.

After two rounds of K 7, P 1, I thought why shouldn't an angel have a pattern around the bottom of its skirt? A diamond would be nice, I thought. I didn't want to carry the pattern-wool for as many as seven stitches, so decided to have the single purled stitch in the pattern-color too. Not purled right away, of course; joining in a new color with a purled stitch (unless you are after a particular effect) looks amateurish. For the first pattern-round I knitted three stitches of blue and one stitch of white around. (All I had for white was some deadwhite synthetic—for goodness' sake where did I get THAT? Oh yes; a new knit shop had opened up and I wanted to encourage them, and they carried no real wool of any color I liked.) The pattern was therefore in a rather thicker yarn, and I must admit that it looked acceptable. (Patterns in a thicker wool stand out nicely; it is in thinner wool that they look spidery and tend to disappear.) On the second pattern-row I of course purled the single rib-stitch. The pattern took five rounds—quite a simple diamond—and after it I decreased one stitch in each of the seven ribs (49 stitches), and continued in blue, remembering to knit the first stitches in the purl ribs for the first round. One stitch was decreased in every knit rib every seven rounds until the whole contraption was down to 21 stitches. Then I made a hole—(yarn over, K 2 together) at each side, changed to all-knit, and worked a final ten rounds, the last of which consisted of K 2 together around. The wool was broken, threaded through the last 10 stitches, pulled tight, and fastened off for the top of the head. Into the head I popped a spruce-cone, wrapped a piece of wool tightly and murderously around below it for the neck, and made about 4″ of idiot-cord (see Appendix) which I pulled through the two holes for the arms.

We considered the angel dubiously, and decided it would come all right on the night, with the help of judicious blocking, a paper cone, perhaps, wire through the arms, and some form of hair. Already it stood up nicely on its ribbed and patterned skirt.

"Looks rather like a hat for a dolly," remarked the old man. So it did.

Soon I shall make a monster angel on 84 stitches—or more—at 5 stitches to 1″. There will be no holes for the arms; cautious drilling with a large knitting-needle makes quite respectable holes which may later be persuaded back to their original texture. I will put all manner of color-patterns round the skirt—trees, stars, perhaps even small angels. I shall give it to a grandchild for Christmas, and after Twelfth Night it can wear the angel as a hat for the rest of the winter.

MY HEART is not really in the designing of Christmas trivia, because my brain is designing a sock-heel.

Do you knit for one of those men equipped with a gimlet or auger under each heel, with which he succeeds in making holes in his socks just beyond the area of nylon heel-strengthening? I do. I have to put neat troublesome darns at this spot, after searching through all his boots and shoes for nails.

Now I think I've come up with a dodge to defeat him. It entails making a kind of pointed spur which reaches out under the foot from the heel-flap, and which is completed before the nylon for the heel-turning is severed.

Start the heel-flap as usual, on half the stitches of the leg, joining in nylon yarn. When there are as many rows as stitches (say 28—many of his socks are on 56 stitches), turn the heel, but differently from the usual way:

Decrease 1 st at the beginning of the first row so that there is an uneven number of stitches. Knit to within 1 stitch of the center-stitch (in this case 13 stitches), slip 1, K 2 together, psso (double-decrease). Knit to end. Purl 1 row. Repeat these two rows, making a double-decrease at the center of the knit row, until one-quarter of the stitches remain (in this case, seven). Now return to normal; knit up stitches along the sides of this odd heel-flap, and continue around, sans nylon. Since there are more stitches than usual, I like to decrease one stitch at each side *every* round for the instep, instead of every second round. Finish the foot in your usual way.

The completed sock will look slightly different below the shoe-line, as it has rather a humpbacked heel, but once it is on the foot it will conform nicely, and, I'm pretty sure, confound those grinding heels.*

YESTERDAY WE SAW A LYNX.

We had canoed up an arm of the lake to where it became swampy and was blocked by a beaverdam. We unloaded the motor and other heavy stuff onto a convenient clummock and dragged the canoe over the dam. We crossed a pond, dragged over a second dam, and found ourselves in a small black

---

*FOOTNOTE: this heel is wearing well so far.

lake about the size of Trafalgar Square, surrounded by swamps and steep sprucegrown shores. There were some fine pitcher-plants, and we surely both thought here lives the grandaddy of all giant fish, undisturbed since the beaver built their lodges, which was a long time ago; their roofs were impenetrably grown with moss and grass.

We were wrong, however. The Northerns in this isolated lakelet were stunted, and very dark from the moory water. The Old Man said their food-supply was probably poor.

But, nosing our way into the swamp to look at pitcher-plants, what should we hear and see but a grunt, a splash, and a flash of dun-colored pelt with two furry ears at one end and a stub of a tail at the other. Off he bounced through the swamp, galumphing from clump to tussock to clummock until he scampered up and out of sight into the forest.

The question as to what he was doing there in the first place was soon answered; with loud quacks and squawks a mallard duck flew up. The lynx had been planning a little lunch.

We had *our* little lunch under the trees on an island in the swamp. The Old Man drew a portrait of the canoe and I made some watercolors of three unknown flower-seeds, then we dragged over the two dams, and went to fishing, well-content with our day.

Don't ever think that I am not knitting busily much of the time. Now that I have those spur-heels off my mind I am finishing the Christmas Angel-Hat, and am right back in the Dark Ages B.C.N.—Before Circular Needles, that is.

Having foolishly done what no knitter should ever do—left home without a 16″ #5 needle—I find myself in a bind, as I am engaged in color-pattern knitting where the wool *must* be carried loosely. This is practically impossible to do if you are holding your work scrunched up so as not to slide off three sock-needles. I have 96 stitches on four 7″ needles, and am carrying two colors. Blankety-Blank, as Edwardian authors would say.

I stopped knitting after about two inches and gave my powerful mind to the matter with the following result:

If you have too many stitches for four needles, and no circular needle at hand, with sewing-needle and wool run a thread through the lower edge of the work and pull tight.

That fixes *that* problem, and I wish I had thought of it fifty years ago. As the piece of knitting lengthens it will probably become advisable to bunch it up with a rubber band, or something, but by that time I'll be at home with my extensive stable of circular needles.

The more you do a thing, the more ways you find of doing it—if you keep an open mind, that is. Quite often the new ways are improvements.

For instance, I pretty invariably cast on by the longtail method where one starts by making a slipknot over the righthand needle. In making a circular article I am annoyed—very slightly, but nevertheless annoyed—by this knot, which I find hard to disguise neatly and effectively. I have tried to eliminate the knot, and have succeeded, and there's one more crumpled roseleaf banished forever:

Simply lay the wool over the righthand needle where it will form the first stitch. Grasp the wool-ends with the left hand, spread thumb and forefinger between them, and proceed as usual. The knot is done away with and the join much neater.

That is the last entry. The weather broke next day, with spectacular high winds and troubled waters. We were up and packed by 8 A.M., and just made it back to the faithful car through high seas and whitecaps. Tremble tremble, but we made it.

One more small Christmas item has been dreamed up since then, and may interest you if you like to decorate your tree with oranges, apples, limes, and lemons, or even a particularly beautiful saved Easter egg. The problem arises of how to attach them. To tie a string around them is practically impossible. If you pierce them with a nail or kitchen match to which to tie a string, they go bad before their time, and fall squishily to the floor. We have used wire nets and other makeshifts, but this year we shall use knitted nets, which are described on the next page.

PITHY DIRECTIONS:
NET FOR FRUIT.

Cast on 6 stitches by Emily Ocker's method and put two of them on each of three needles. Work around.

Rnd 1. *K 1, make 2 by putting 2 backward loops over righthand needle. Rep from * around. (18 sts)

Rnds 2, 3, and 4. Knit around.

Rnd 5. *K 1, make 1 by putting backward loop over righthand needle, drop 2. Rep from * around. (12 sts)

Rnd 6. Knit around, break wool, fasten last st securely to first. Thread 15″ of contrasting wool through all sts, and knot. Remove needles, if you haven't already done so. Pop in an orange, and let the stitches drop as far as they will go. For smaller orange, omit rnd 4.

By using different-colored wool to thread through the stitches, you will be able to take the orange out more easily when the time comes. If you use dark green, it will tend to disappear against the green of the tree.

I used knitting worsted and very large wooden needles—size 10. Try using metallic thread after you have become used to handling such large needles with so few stitches. Do not become ambitious and try a shopping net made by this method; it won't work. The threads will catch on things and pull out into surprising loops.

STAR.

Any wool you like, firmly knitted. 1 pr. needles. Cast on 55 sts. (5 times 11). Work in garter-stitch.

Row 1. K 4, sl 1, K 2 tog, psso, (K 8, sl 1, K 2 tog, psso) 4 times, K 4.

Row 2. K 3, sl 1, K 2 tog, psso, (K 6, sl 1, K 2 tog, psso) 4 times, K 3.

Row 3. K 2, sl 1, K 2 tog, psso, (K 4, sl 1, K 2 tog, psso) 4 times, K 2.

Row 4. K 1, sl 1, K 2 tog, psso, (K 2, sl 1, K 2 tog, psso) 4 times, K 1.

Row 5. (sl 1, K 2 tog, psso) 5 times. Thread wool through last 5 sts, pull tight, sew up short 5-row edge. Block severely, pinning out each point as sharply as possible. Leave to dry. For fatter star on more sts, insert K rows between decreasing rows when total sts have been reduced to a little less than half.

TREE.

Any wool you like, firmly knitted. 1 pr. needles. Cast on 77 sts. (7 × 11). Work in garter-stitch.

Row 1. K 4, sl 2 tog, K 1, p 2 sso, (K 8, sl 2, K 1, p 2 sso) 6 times, K 4.

Row 2. Knit, purling all double-decrease sts if you like.

Row 3. K 3, sl 2 tog, K 1, p 2 sso, (K 6, sl 2, K 1, p 2 sso) 6 times, K 3.

Row 4. Rep. row 2.

Row 5. K 2, sl 2 tog, K 1, p 2 sso, (K 4, sl 2, K 1, P 2 sso) 6 times, K 2.

Row 6. Rep, row 2.

*K 14, turn, K back. K 11, turn, K back. K 8, turn, K back. Cast on 4. K 9, turn, K back. K 1 row, Rep from *. K to center and weave halves together.

ANGEL.

Any wool you like, firmly knitted around on 4 needles. Cast on 56 P 1 rnd and work in rib of K 7, P 1, for 7 rnds, (putting in star after two rnds). *Decr 7 sts evenly-spaced around. Work 6 rnds. Rep from * until 21 sts remain. Work 10 rnds even. K 2 tog around. Finish off, insert rabble of wool-ends for head. Wind wool firmly around neck. Insert short piece of idiot-cord for arms. Attach ravelled wool for hair. Embroider or paint features.

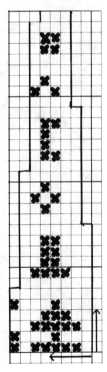

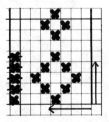

Star Graph   *Large Angel Graph*

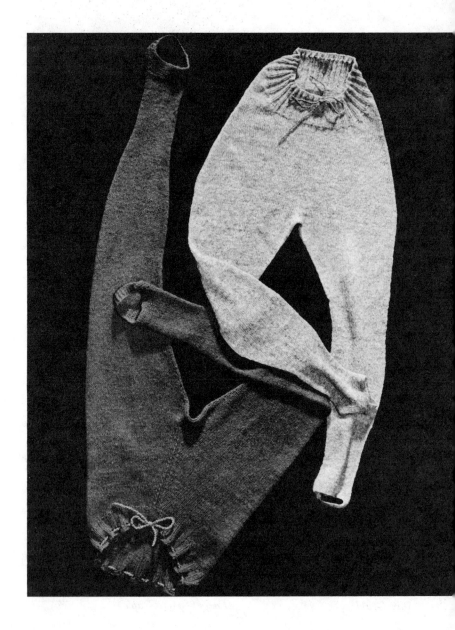

SEPTEMBER

Nether Garments

SEPTEMBER IS THE LOGICAL BEGINNING of the year. Summer heat is nearly past, the weather begins to brisken up, schools open their doors to siphon our beloved young out of the house for longer or shorter periods, adult activity starts to stir, and Mother forms good resolutions and makes lists.

Top your list with a resolution to initiate all children, M and F, into the mysteries and fascinations of knitting.

An excellent first project is a garter-stitch pot-holder. It will probably turn out thin, lumpy, sleazy, and full of holes, but it is a small project, comparatively soon finished, and very easy to make much of.

Provide suitable and encouraging tools and materials. Few things are sadder than to see an eager and willing child struggling with heavy 10″ aluminum pins and some leftover fine wool. Invest in two pairs of short light plastic needles, size 5 or 6, in two colors, and some of that variegated wool. Yes; I know that the results may be deplorable, but children are fascinated by variegated wool. Deal out one needle of each color; this will be of great help when the time comes to knit and purl alternate rows. If a needle is lost, you will have two in reserve.

When the discouraged child brings its project to the expert to have a dropped stitch retrieved, always add a few free stitches, or even perhaps a row or two, to speed completion. Then hang the pot-holder up behind the stove, and use it, and use it, and *use* it. It won't be your most efficient pot-holder—it will give you many a burned hand—but use it. It won't even be necessary to comment on its excellence or beauty every time you use it; you will be noticed, and the fact that it will soon become shabby, worn, and beat-up will be the best thanks and encouragement you can give. Soon its successor will be cast on.

One of my regrets is that when our kids went through the stage of giving me pepper-and-salt sets from a shop which for some reason they liked to patronize, I didn't use them. They were small, awkward, and in eternal need of re-filling, so I pretended to make a collection of them in the glass-cupboard. Nobody was fooled by this; they kept trying, year after year, with the new models, and I, foolish wayward woman, stayed with my original tried-and-true pepper-and-salts. Eheu. Some memories gladden a mother's heart; others she regrets for the rest of her life.

Sit and knit with your child; while it perfects its pot-holder you can knit a fine reward—a pair of longies.

Every time a new knitting-magazine comes out I scan it hopefully for a sign of truly organically-designed pants, slacks, or tights. In vain. Even baby-leggings are made in two flat pieces and sewn together. Wouldn't you think that such a very circular piece of work would bring the term "circular needle" to the designers' minds? Not on your tintype.

Let us be the first on the block, then, yea, the first in the town, the county, the State, to make these useful garments the way I'm sure Providence intended them to be made, on circular needles: and when too small for that, on a set of four sock-needles. The main thing is to avoid all seams, which pop inconveniently, especially in a garment which has to have feet constantly thrust into it. Besides, sewn seams are rarely an embellishment, and sometimes downright ugly.

For a start, let us take baby-leggings, for which you can leaf back to page 25. Make a pair, and they may well spur you on to try such a comfortable and convenient garment in larger sizes, or even for yourself. For ballet-dancers and skaters they are mandatory, and even the shy housewife likes to slip them on under her slacks to go to the store on exceptionally cold days. I have been known to pull them on under a housedress, add boots, my warm coat, and woolly cap and mittens, and trot comfortably to the A&P, looking (almost) like everybody else.

We do all like to look like everybody else, especially kids. What is better for wearing under their long sweaters or attentuated skirts in winter than knitted tights? They are faster to make than you would think; actually a pair weighs no more than an average sweater, and thus entails no more knitting. Buy as much wool, therefore, as you would for an average sweater: five 4oz skeins of knitting worsted, or less of thinner wool. Hunt up a 16″ and a 24″ circular needle, and a set of 4 needles of a size to give you a suitable GAUGE in the wool you have chosen (here the sales clerk can be of great help) and *Make a Swatch.*

The swatch should be at least 4″ wide, and almost as long—in fact the size of a smallish pot-holder, but in stocking-stitch. If you happen to need a pot-holder you can border it with garter-stitch to prevent it from curling. The point is that the swatch must be large enough for you to be able to measure off 3″ in the middle without becoming involved in selvedges; selvedges are hopeless for measuring GAUGE. Place two pins exactly 3″ apart horizontally in the fabric of the swatch, and meticulously and honestly count the number of stitches and half-stitches between the pins. Divide the number of stitches by three, and the result will be *your* GAUGE of stitches to 1″.

If there are 12 stitches, your GAUGE is 4 stitches to 1″.
If there are 13 stitches, your GAUGE is 4.333 recurring stitches to 1″.
If there are 14 stitches, your GAUGE is 4.666 recurring stitches to 1″.
If there are 15 stitches, your GAUGE is 5 stitches to 1″.
If there are 16 stitches, your GAUGE is 5.333 recurring stitches to 1″.
If there are 17 stitches, your GAUGE is 5.666 recurring stitches to 1″.
If there are 18 stitches, your GAUGE is 6 stitches to 1″.

I could go on like this forever. Let us hope that you have 12, 15, or 18 stitches to 3″, which, being interpreted, means 4, 5, or 6 stitches to 1″ respectively. If you have any number not exactly divisible by three, and are frightened by decimals, change needle-sizes until you have straightened things out.

The reason for measuring 3″ and dividing by three is to save you from the temptation to cheat by one-half or one-third of a stitch when measuring

1″. This is liable to play old hob with the measurements of a finished garment. I hasten to add that I was not resistant to temptation in my youth, and devised the 3″ method to save me from myself. An inexactitude of one-half or one-third of a stitch over 3″ has proved to matter hardly at all on a finished garment but over 1″ it can mean disaster.

Having thus established your GAUGE for current conditions—conditions of wool-thickness, needle-size, and state of mind—write it down in the margin, and take some measurements.

Measure your ankle, knee, thigh, hips, and waist, multiply them by your GAUGE, and write down the answers in the spaces provided. All measurements are of circumference; measurements of length will be decided by trying-on.

Ankle . . . .″		= . . . . .sts.
Knee . . . .″	multiplied by . . .	= . . . . .sts.
Thigh . . . .″	(*your* GAUGE of stitches to 1″)	= . . . . .sts.
Hips . . . .″		= . . . . .sts.
Waist . . . .″		= . . . . .sts.

Adult tights are best made from the bottom up, as the union of the legs is more anatomical when it runs fore-and-aft. (For diapered babies it is better to have the crotch-seam running sideways.) Work both legs at once, if you prefer, and soon start trying them on to ascertain the proper length.

It is best, I think, to make them without feet, since the sock-part would need more frequent washing than the rest. If you want them with feet, cast on by the invisible method (see Appendix) and add the feet last.

So!

Starting at the ankle, with the sock-needles, cast on the number of stitches you have calculated. Work about 1″ in border-texture, be it ribbing, garter-stitch, moss-stitch, or whatever. Change to stocking-stitch, and work around until the piece is about 5″ long. Now make an elegant shaping for the calf, and change to the 16″ circular needle in the process:

Mark two stitches for the center-back, and increase one stitch each side of them by any method you please. I like to "make" them by putting backward loops over the righthand needle, and have trained myself to twist this loop over my left forefinger for the first increase, and over my left thumb for the second (see Appendix). This makes the increases absolutely symmetrical, but you don't have to do it if you don't want to. Increase any way you wish, but be sure to keep the two stitches between the increases in a straight vertical line. Otherwise your increasing may spiral disconcertingly.

Work two rounds plain, and make two more increases. Continue thus, increasing every third round, until you have the number of stitches which you calculated for the knee. Then work straight to the actual knee.

Now start the "inseam"-increasing, which is placed, as you would expect, at the inseam, about one-quarter of the stitches away from the vertical line of the calf-increases. Be sure to have this shaping at the proper place, so that the inseams will face each other: that is to say *beyond* the calf-increase for the right leg, and *before* it for the left leg. Increase at the same rate—two stitches every third round—until you have the number of stitches you calculated for the thigh. Now work straight to the crotch.

These increase-instructions are for a leg of average proportions. For a short sturdy leg you may wish to have the increase-rounds closer together; every second round instead of every third. For a slender leg they may be four rounds apart. Don't strain the brain too much about all this. Knitted fabric is notoriously stretchable, and small errors of judgment will soon be dissipated when the leggings are on the legs.

Before knitting the legs together, try them on carefully to be sure the length is right. The stitches for the crotch are then put on shortish pieces of wool, and in order to calculate them correctly we subtract half the hip-stitches from the stitches of one thigh. Generally this is around 3″ worth of stitches, or about a dozen, give or take half a dozen. Much depends on the relative proportions of the individual thighs and hips.

Now put all the stitches (except those on threads for the crotch) on the 24″ needle and work around for about ten rounds.

Next, shape for the waist. Mark two sets of two stitches, one at each side, and *de*crease one stitch each side of them every third round. A good efficient decrease is worked as follows: Work to within one stitch of the two marked stitches, knit 2 together, SSK. (You may also mark one stitch if you wish, work to within one stitch of it, slip 1, Knit 2 together, and pass slipped stitch over. Or slip 2 together, knit 1, pass two slipped stitches over. You may even knit three together if you want to. Just take care that the decrease-lines are strictly vertical.) By the time you are down to the number of stitches you have calculated for the waist the depth of your knitting should be enough. If not, work a few more rounds until you are just about at the belly-button. (For the slender, the decreases may well be placed at front and back.)

The waist-back is now shaped. Put one-quarter of the stitches on a piece of wool at center-front, and work back-and-forth on the remaining three-quarters, leaving one more stitch at the end of each row on the needle, thus working on progressively fewer and fewer stitches. When half the waist stitches remain, work around on all stitches for about $2\frac{1}{2}''$ of knit 2, purl 2, rib. You may put in eyelets, if you like, by working yarn over, purl two together in the purl ribs.

Cast off loosely in ribbing, weave the crotch, and sew broad elastic under the instep. Thread narrow elastic through the eyelets at waist. Done.

Sometimes I like to shape the lower edges to dip down at each ankle, so that they cover more of the foot. To achieve this I cast on about 24 more stitches (a multiple of 4) than I have reckoned for the ankle. As I work the border I decrease those extra stitches, diametrically opposed, two at each ankle, every second round. The two resulting points are united under the foot by a shortish piece of wide elastic, or by a strip of knitting.

If you want a pair of narrow *slacks,* start them with the knee-stitches; wider pants may be started with the thigh-stitches and worked straight to the crotch. You may also branch out into bell-bottoms by starting with as many stitches as you wish, and gradually *de*creasing to the point of the crotch. But this I count as Fashion, or Knitting-ephemera, and, as such, outside my range of interest or desire to execute.

There is nothing to stop you from inserting color-patterns in leggings—on a shapely and slender leg they are an embellishment—but be sure to carry the wool loosely on the inside. And another thing; be consistent, in a given round, in carrying one color in the right hand in the U.S. style, and the second color in the left hand in the Continental style. In some patterns, where the majority of stitches of one color varies very much from round to round, it is permissible to change the hand which holds a main color, but only at the beginning of a round.

This may seem to you to be a pettifogging and niggling piece of advice, but let me give two examples of the possible results of overlooking it:

As a super-labor-of-love I once knitted the old man a pair of Norwegian black-and-white elaborately-patterned ski-stockings (he likes to do his cross-country skiing in knickerbockers). When the time came to work the heel and instep I decided to make the lower—or invisible—part of the foot in vertical one-stitch black-and-white stripes, as a way of carrying the wool without the trouble of knitting patterns where nobody would see them. Lazy, but canny.

The stockings were completed, accepted, worn with pride, and are still in use. But wash them, block them as I may, I cannot eradicate some uneven patches in those vertical stripings under the feet. For years this bothered me, but now I know the reason; I had innocently changed hands with my black and white wools from time to time, and my hands must carry at two different tensions, causing one color to predominate over the other, and to vary, depending on the hand in which it was held.

The second example is more visible and shameful. I must have done the same thing without noticing it when making the ski-sweater for my second television series on knitting. There were some rounds of alternate stitches in one of the patterns, and I suppose I changed hands, with the result that there is an awful line of darkness on the righthand side of the chest. This sweater was photographed for "Knitting Without Tears" where it sits enshrined for evermore. Perhaps knitters will take comfort in the fact that even the Busy Knitter is human. But one thing I'll do; I'll go after it. Next chance I get I'll either tighten the dark wool or loosen the light one in that particular row.

I know why it happened, too. The 13-week series, which was watched in such a leisurely fashion, one half-hour a week, was made in just two weeks, sometimes with three lessons taped in one day. One day the cameras threw their hands in, too, which made things even more hectic. (And once the cat

KLINE got himself lost in the prop-room!) I was constrained to practice some justified deception, in that I actually had $2\frac{1}{2}$ sweaters going at once, so that I could pick up and work on the one most appropriate to the lesson being taped. Then home I would go, and knit my fingers to the bone to catch up, and appear next day, bland and smirking, with a piece of knitting to which—ostensibly—a full week's work had been added.

Talking of uneven knitting, are you one of those people—numerous as the sands on the shore—who purl more tightly than they knit, or vice versa? Does your 2-needle stocking-stitch look rather interestingly uneven, and do the ridges on the wrong side clot in pairs? Find out whether it is knit or purl which you work more tightly, and take a size larger needle for it. In extreme cases, try a needle two sizes larger. (Circular knitting, of course, obviates this problem.)

I'm embarrassed to mention it, but truth will out; how often have you noticed that a sweater in a *knitting book* displays this rather unprofessional idiosyncrasy? True; it's not commonly met with, but it's not unknown. Wouldn't you think they'd take the trouble to use needles of two different sizes, or else pass the job on to a more even knitter? Perhaps they didn't even notice the blooper, or they don't know of a way to cope with it? Don't place unlimited credence in us knitting-instruction-writers, or believe everything in print to be infallible. We do our best, but it may easily be that *your* best is better than ours. Don't hesitate to improve on us.

PITHY DIRECTIONS FOR TIGHTS, CHILDREN AND ADULTS.

GAUGE 5 sts to 1".

MATERIALS: 3–5 skeins knitting worsted, depending on size. 1 16", 1 24" circular needle, 1 set of 4 needles of a size to give *you* correct GAUGE. First take some measurements:

A(nkle)... inches		A .... sts
K(nee) ... inches		K .... sts
T(high)... inches	multiplied by your GAUGE =	T .... sts
H(ips).... inches	(... sts to 1")	H .... sts
W(aist) ... inches		W .... sts

CAST ON A. ... .sts. Work 14 ridges of garter-st. Join, and work around on 4 needles for about 5", or distance to calf. Mark 2 sts at center-back and inc. 1 st each side of them every 3rd rnd until you have K. . . .sts. Change to 16" needle when sts permit. Work even to knee. Mark 2 sts at inseam, $\frac{1}{4}$ of the sts beyond calf-increase for R leg and $\frac{1}{4}$ of the sts before calf-increase for L leg. Inc at these points in same manner until you have T. . . .sts. Work even to crotch. Subtract half of H. . . .sts from T. . . .sts. The difference, ...sts, is put on pieces of wool at inseam. Work around on all H. . . .sts on 24" needle for about 10 rnds. Mark 2 sts at sides, (or at center-front and center-back), and *de*crease 1 st each side of them every 3rd round until you have W. . . .sts. When about 2" shy of desired length, place $\frac{1}{4}$ of stitches on piece of wool at center-front. Work back-and-forth on remaining sts, leaving 1 st on needle at end of each row, thus working progressively less sts until $\frac{1}{2}$ of waist sts remain. Work around on all W. . . .sts in K 2 P 2, rib for $2\frac{1}{2}"$. Cast off loosely. Weave crotch. Put wide elastic under feet and narrow elastic at waist.

OCTOBER

Open-Collared Pullover

OCTOBER; THE MONTH when knitting really starts coming into its own again.

Conditions are favorable, for one thing. The sun is once more welcome to shine in at the south windows, and as the sunshiny patch moves across the floor the cats move with it, basking and stretching. Their food-bowls have been moved indoors, and they do not sally forth unless obliged.

The yard is bedded down for the winter, and the outdoors no longer beckons the sedentary knitter except for an hour or so at noon.

The wooden wall clock ticks slightly unevenly—I must straighten it—and the kettle sings on the stove.

I am working on one of my early brainchildren—an open-collared shirt, currently called, I think, a golf-shirt—which was sidetracked about fifteen years ago as being too complicated for comprehensible directions. Since then my direction-writing has progressed, as well as competence with wool and circular needle, and I trust that this design will now prove moderately easy to understand, although slightly on the convoluted side. Incorporated in it you will find what I believe to be a brand-new technique—the Idiot-Cord knitted-in border.

Start in the usual fashion by *Making a Swatch,* and then by measuring yourself at your widest, and multiplying the inches by your GAUGE. The result is the number of stitches to cast on for the body, and in my case this *Key-number* is 200 (5 stitches to 1″ times 40″ around). This number has been broken down into percentages; no matter how many stitches you have, the same percentages apply.

Cast on the key-number of 200 stitches on a 24″ circular needle, and work around to the underarm. You may care to cast on ten (5%) fewer stitches (190), and then increase them, evenly-spaced, across the back only, after 2″ or 3″. This will cause the lower edge to fit snugly, and the lower back to blouse slightly.

There is a cosy homemade formula for doing this which you may find useful. It spaces the ten stitches evenly across the back, and keeps them at a respectful distance from the two side-seam stitches, which may prove a convenience later on:

First divide the stitches into front and back; 99 on front and 89 on back, separated by a seam-stitch on either side. Mark the seam-stitches with safety-pins. Into the 89 stitches of the back you must insert the ten extra stitches. Subtract 1 from 10, which leaves 9. Divide 89 by 9, which yields 9 and 8 over. First knit half of the 8 extra stitches—4—and Make 1 by putting a backward loop over the right-hand needle (see Appendix). Now keep knitting 9 and making 1 across until you are within 4 stitches of the second seam-stitch. Ten stitches will have been increased, regularly-spaced, and the seam-stitch safety-pins will be in stitches #1 and #101, where they belong, at a safe distance from the first and last increases. Move the safety-pins up as you go along; they will prove useful friends and companions.

If you want to make your sweater fit superlatively, you may care to insert a few Short Rows, (See Appendix) fairly evenly-spaced, across the back, as you proceed—every 4″ or 5″, or about three times.

The timid or beginning knitter may feel free to disregard the previous three paragraphs, but the rapidly-developing expert may read, mark, and inwardly digest.

When the body is worked up to the armholes, place the underarm stitches on pieces of wool on either side. They will consist of 8% of the 200 stitches of body, or 16 on each side. Make sure that the stitches of back and front are equal—84 for back; 84 for front. Set the body aside, and tackle the short sleeves.

Now is a favorable moment to introduce you to Idiot-Cord border. Both sleeve-bands make use of it, and you may as well understand it thoroughly before it pops up again in the front-placket and collar.

Idiot-Cord, as you perhaps know, consists of a very skinny tube of only three stitches. Tantamount to impossible of achievement on three needles holding one stitch each(!), it is cunningly contrived by knitting the same three stitches on double-pointed needles, over and over again in the same direction, pulling the wool so firmly across the back between the end of the third stitch and the beginning of the first that it blends into and becomes the fabric of the tube. See Appendix.

The same technique may be used for a knitted-in border on the lower edge of the 10-stitch sleeve-bands which are worked sideways.

Cast on 10 stitches. *Knit 7, and put wool forward. Slip the last 3 stitches as if to purl. Turn, knit 10. Repeat from *. Do not pull the wool as firmly as you would for Idiot-Cord itself, as this might produce an undesirably tight edge. Continue until there are 60 ridges of garter-stitch, or 30% of 200. Weave, or skillfully sew, the ends together.

With a 16″ circular needle knit up 60 stitches along the un-idiotic side of the band, and knit about 4″, or to the length *you* wish for a short sleeve, increasing 2 stitches at underarms 3 times about 5 rounds apart, to end up with 66 stitches or 33% of 200. Sleeves may be long if you wish; for them I commend you to your own sterling commonsense.

Having finished body and sleeves to the underarm, you will find that the contemplative period of this sweater is at an end. From now on, everything will happen at once.

Assemble Body and Sleeves:

Put 16 stitches at the underarm of each sleeve on pieces of wool, and place all remaining stitches (168 of body and 50 of each sleeve) on the 24″ needle, matching underarms. Work 2 rounds on all 268 stitches to calm your nerves and embark on:

Neck-Placket Opening:

From now on you will be working back-and-forth on the circular needle. Mark the dead-center of the front, which, in the case of a 200-stitch sweater, will fall between stitches #42 and #43 of the 84 front-stitches. Fine; you can use a ring-marker if you wish (although I prefer a safety-pin). When you have

knitted to within 5 stitches of this mid-point, *Cast on* 10 stitches by means
of 10 backward loops over the right-hand needle. *Turn.* K 10. Continue on
The Wrong Side, in *Purl,* until you are within 5 stitches of the marker. Knit
7, wool forward, slip 3 stitches as if to purl. (This is the beginning of the
Right-hand Idiot-Cord edge.) **Turn.* Knit to within 3 stitches of end, wool
forward, slip 3 stitches as if to purl. (This is the beginning of the *other* piece
of Idiot-Cord on the *left-hand,* or placket, side.) *Turn,* Knit 10, purl to within
10 stitches of end, knit 7, wool forward, slip 3 stitches as if to purl. Repeat
from *. This is a mind-boggling operation, hard to describe, but, I hope, easy
to follow blindly until you get the hang of it. You will be performing it right
up to the neckline, so get the hang of it you must, and fast, because the
shoulder-shaping is now going to start.

Raglan Shoulder-Shaping:

When 8 rows have been worked after the union of body and sleeves, mark
4 single stitches, two on the front, two on the back, by placing safety-pins
in the first and last stitches of the front, and the first and last stitches of the
back.

You will decrease 2 stitches at each of these four points every second row
(on the knit row) until the sleeve-stitches have been eliminated, and about
68 stitches (roughly 33% of 200) remain for the neck and collar.

How you decrease is a matter of individual taste. Sometimes I slip 1, knit
2 together, and pass the slipped stitch over them (sl 1, K 2 tog, psso), sometimes I slip 2 together as if to knit, knit 1, and pass the 2 slipped stitches
over it. (Sl 2, K 1, p 2 sso). The former makes a small teepee of the 3 stitches
involved; the latter causes the center stitch to swallow the two outside stitches
and form a chain running up the line of decreasing. In either case the three
stitches unite to form one, and this one *must* be the marked stitch, and the
center-stitch of the following decrease. Thus the decrease-line makes a straight
diagonal, which does not veer in one direction or the other, as is sometimes
the case when knitters do not keep their heads.

The decreasing on the model shown was achieved by marking *two* stitches
at each decrease-point (one from the body and one from the sleeve) and working
SSK to the right of them and K 2 together to the left.

There you go then, busy as a bee, making Idiot-Cord edges at the end of each row, keeping the 10 edge-stitches in garter-stitch on a stocking-stitch fabric, decreasing at each of the four points every second row, and *at the same time*, as the knitting-books put it, not forgetting the. . .

Buttonholes:

These should be on the right side, about every tenth garter-stitch ridge. (For directions, see p. 80.)

If you are as lazy-minded as I am, you will space your buttonholes by divine inspiration, about 10 ridges apart with the first one at five ridges. If they don't come out quite right, you will make the terminal one a modest loop with a small pearl button to match it on the other side.

On the model you will notice that I have increased the field of garter-stitch by one stitch every fifth ridge. *You* certainly don't have to do this if it fusses you.

When all the sleeve-stitches have been swallowed up by the raglan-decreasing, you have arrived at the neck. Things have shaped up nicely, and it's time to think about the collar.

First eliminate 5 stitches at each end by *working only the three Idiot-Cord stitches for five rows, slipping the third stitch, knitting the next stitch (one of the garter-stitches from the placket-border) and passing the slipped stitch over it. Replace the three stitches on the left-hand needle and repeat from * five times in all. Work across and repeat at the other side. This makes a neat professional job of the neck-placket and is well worth the trouble. Now we are in the clear. All that remains is:

The Collar:

This is worked on the remaining stitches, back-and-forth in garter-stitch with the faithful Idiot-Cord border at each end. There should be about 68 stitches, or approximately 33% of 200. Increase 1 stitch at the beginning of each row, by M 1, right after the Idiot-Cord, to make nice-looking collar-points. When the collar is long enough (about $3\frac{1}{2}''$ or 20 ridges), perform the magic trick of. . .

Idiot-Cord Casting-off:

Could you imagine yet *another* way to cast off? This is really the same trick you used for those 5 stitches at each neck-front: Starting at left-hand collar-point, * knit the first two stitches, slip the third as if to knit, knit the fourth stitch, and pass the slipped stitch over it. (Or, better, SSK. See Appendix.) Replace the three stitches on the left-hand needle, and repeat from * along entire collar-edge. At the right-hand point weave the last three stitches to the three edge-stitches.

If you want Phoney Seams, see Appendix,

Weave underarms (see p. 48, and Appendix).

Tack down cast-on stitches at bottom of placket.

Add Afterthought Pockets (see Appendix) if and where wanted.

Decide what kind of a border you want for the lower edge of body. For a long sweater, many people like a hem, as given at the end of the March chapter.

You may also make an Idiot-Cord lower border to match the sleeves, as is shown on the model: cast on 10 and keep one edge for the Idiot-Cord. Along the other edge, *as you knit,* knit the last stitch together with one cast-on stitch from the lower edge of body. Of course you may start with the border as on the sleeves, but when I begin a sweater from the bottom I rarely know in advance what kind of a border I shall prefer when the sweater is finished.

A nice job, right?

CAN YOU GUESS what frustration is nagging at me? *I don't like to work back-and-forth unless there is no way of avoiding it.* That's all I have been brooding on during the latter reaches of this sweater—*how* can I do it round and round on a circular needle, neck-opening, collar, and all?

(The Old Man, on reading what follows, said, "They will sue you." I said, "Why?". He said, "They will be bald." I said, *"What?"* He said, "They will tear out their hair.")

Let's face it; I did make one round and round. At the beginning of the placket I suddenly cast on a pouch of about 30 stitches (sufficient to make a faced-back lap-over) which I cut when I came to the neck. I can give directions for cutting without a pang—many of my designs call for cutting, and people expect it of me—but directions for knitting a great blister of 30 stitches in a piece of circular knitting I will not give. Such cruelty to the innocent knitter must not be countenanced; I must think up another device.

A faced-back opening appealed to me—especially if combined with a faced collar, and hemmed sleeves and lower edge. In fine Shetland wool at 6 stitches to 1″ it would look classic, rich, and lovely. In a sweater *started from the top* the stitches of the placket facing would be no bother. They could be abandoned on a piece of wool at the bottom of the neck-opening, and worked later to make a complete facing all around the neck.

A faced collar could be started on a circular needle, and the edge woven at the latter end, couldn't it? It could, and we will prove it.

We will start at the absolute top of the garment—the collar-edge. Take it from one who has calculated and experimented that the width of the collar is 85% of the width of the body. So 85% of the circumference of the body will equal the combined widths of collar and collar-facing.

This brings us again to our old friend, body-width, or *Key-number* of stitches.

I am using real Shetland wool, with which I like to knit at a GAUGE of 18 stitches to 3″, or 6 stitches to 1″. (I use a #2 needle; you may need a thicker or a thinner one.)

My sweater is to be 40″ around. I multiply 40 by my GAUGE of 6 stitches to 1″, and arrive at the *key-number* of 240 stitches—a fine flexible number, divisible in many various ways.

85% of 240? Easy for some of us.

For others: Subtract 10%. 240 − 24 (10%) = 216. 216 − 12 (5%; $\frac{1}{2}$ of 10%) = 204. For collar and collar-facing combined we will cast on 204. Look up Invisible Casting-on in the Appendix and cast on 204 stitches by this method on a 24″ circular needle. Join, and work two rounds, taking enormous care that the stitches are not twisted on the needle.

Now mark 2 stitches at the beginning and two stitches at the halfway point, with 100 stitches between them. These will be at either end of the faced, lined, or double-collar, and we will decrease 1 stitch each side of them every second round:

*Knit to within 1 stitch of marked stitches, K 2 together, SSK.

* Knit to within 1 stitch of opposite marked stitches, K 2 together, SSK. Knit 1 round. Rep from * until 160 stitches remain.

Why 160? Well, I will tell you. The neck on a sweater of this kind should have approximately 33% of the *key-number* of body-stitches, and 33% of 240 is 80. Since the collar is double, and now has 160 stitches, which is double of 80, we are in a fine position to consider ourselves at the neckline. Do you follow? If not, trust me, and press on. Things are going to become more complicated right away.

Cast off 40 sts (half of 33% of 240) at the exact center of one side of the collar for neck-back. There remain 20 stitches to right and to left of them, plus the 80 neck-stitches on the other side—120 stitches in all. (50% of 240; a fairly insignificant statistic, but a comforting one.) *None* of these stitches will be decreased or eliminated in the next stage of the sweater; you will knit around on them, leaving the cast-off stitches as a pouch. 80 stitches will form the neck, and the remaining pair of twenties will be the two *front-facings*. Right away now, you will start increasing for the. . . .

Raglan Shoulder-Lines:

Keep Calm. Mark 1 stitch at each end of the center 40 stitches of neck-back, plus the two contiguous stitches of the pair of 20 stitches. *When you come to the first group of 3, Make 1, knit stitch number 1, make 1, knit center st, make 1, knit stitch number 3, make 1. (4 stitches increased.) Knit to the opposite group of 3 and repeat this increase. Work one round plain, taking in your stride the fact that your knitting looks lopsided. It should. Repeat from *. Stitches number 1 and 3 of the marked stitches will diverge as raglan-lines, and stitch number 2 will melt away in the sleeve and never be heard from again. You will be increasing 1 stitch on either side of the first and third stitch every second round. Proceed thus, alternating increase-rounds and plain rounds and averting your eyes and mind from the fact that front and back are so offensively uneven.

There are many delightful ways of working a double-increase; no doubt you have your own favorite. I will just mention one that I find particularly attractive, and quote (by kind permission) from Barbara Walker's "Knitting from the Top":

"Double increase #4: knit into back of the stitch in the row below the (marked) stitch (inserting needle downward into the purled head of this stitch on the wrong side), then knit into the back of the (marked) stitch itself, then with left needle draw up the left side loop of the same stitch in the row below, and knit into the back of this strand for the third stitch."

(Nothing can be gained by concealing from you the fact that the raglan-shaping of the model was *not* worked by this method. Your sharp eyes will have spotted a rather pretty wavy line. Without going into harrowing detail I will admit that this section of the sweater was worked from the *bottom up*, and that the *de*creasings were worked singly, every round, three of them in SSK, and then three in K 2 together, alternately. You may care to employ this technique, one of these days. End of honorable confession.)

When the sleeve-stitches between the marked stitches number 60 (i.e. *33%* of 240 minus 8% of 240 for underarms; believe me), put them on pieces of wool at either side. On this same happy and exciting occasion you may put those unattractive 40 surplus stitches at center-front also on a piece of wool when you come to them, which makes a second pouch. You are almost home free.

Keep knitting around, and when you come to the first sleeve, cast on 20 stitches (approximately 8% of 240) for the underarm. As a perfectionist you will cast them on by the Invisible Casting-on method (see Appendix), but if you recoil from this, cast them on any old way, as they will be fairly hidden at the underarm. Proceed to the second sleeve and do likewise, paying no attention to the front-opening stitches as you pass them.

Before you now stretches a period of calm and placid knitting. You should have 240 stitches (give or take a few, possibly) on the 24″ needle, and will work straight to that famous spot, "Desired Length of Body". Styles at present are in such a state of flux that I refuse to specify length, except perhaps to say that a longish sweater is always warm and comfortable—I make mine from 17″–19″ from the underarm down as I have slight personal interest in fashion.

You may insert three or four pairs of short rows across the back (see Appendix), and decrease 10 or 12 stitches evenly-spaced across the back only, 2″–3″ from the lower edge.

Put in Phoney Seams if you wish (see Appendix).

Purl one round to turn the hem, and finish it as at the end of the March chapter.

Pick up the stitches of one sleeve on a 16″ circular needle, pull out the piece of string from the invisibly cast-on stitches, and pick them up too. In all there should be 80 stitches (33% of 240). If you didn't cast on invisibly, knit up 20 stitches from the cast-on section.

Sleeves are now worked to that ephemeral distance, Desired Length. Mine are 8″ long, and are hemmed like the lower edge of the body. I decreased 2 stitches about every inch at the underarm to a total of 64 stitches, but this is optional; it doesn't make a very tidy percentage—something around 25% of 240. Use your judgment combined with your taste in sleeve-widths. I left a full three stitches between the decreases, and then, because I had used invisible casting-on at the underarms, I could drop my Phoney Seam stitch clear down from the bottom of the sleeve to the bottom of the sweater before hooking it up again; a most satisfying tour de force.

Take out the string from the Invisible Casting-on at collar-edge, put collar-back and collar-front each on a straight needle, and weave (see Appendix).

There remains now but that peculiar deformity at neck-front which you will notice, in its raw state, in the illustration. Looks rather like Piglet, really, or perhaps Roo? Run a basting-thread down its exact center, machine-stitch twice each side of the basting, and cut on basting. That's all the cutting there is.

The two cut edges now fold themselves inwards with docility to form the neck-facing. Pick up the orphan stitches left on wool at their lower edges, and work about $3\frac{1}{2}$″ of stocking-stitch, bordering it with 4 stitches of garter-stitch, and ending with 4 ridges of the same. Properly pressed back, the facing will hardly need attaching on the inside, but you may do this if you like—extremely lightly. Judicious tightening of the stitches at the lower point of the opening, and a couple of strategic stitches with a darning-needle will put the final touch to an impressive piece of knitmanship. Non-knitters may take this sweater in their stride, but the true knitting craftsman will gasp and stretch his or her eyes, especially when you reveal that the only purl stitches in the whole thing are in that small invisible bit of lower neck-facing, and the turning-lines for the hems. Actually, on the larger model I didn't even purl for the hems, but worked one super-loose round (Yarn Over, Knit 2, and drop the Yarn Overs in the next round). Stocking-stitch has a slight but delightful tendency to turn at a loose round.

Make three or four neat loops at the edge of the appropriate side of neck-opening, and—you guessed it—sew on buttons to match.

Or lace up the front with Idiot-Cord. Or with a twisted cord, or embellish it with those beautiful Norwegian hooks and eyes.

Now, I WOULD NOT FOR A MOMENT suggest that this is the easiest of sweaters, but I put it to you that its difficulties are more apparent than actual if you keep tight hold upon yourself at the crucial points.

To start with Invisible Casting-on is intimidating only to those who have not yet mastered this technique. Once you have learned it you will not be too startled by its reappearance at the underarms. Practice will soon prove that it is the very fastest of all the castings-on.

Beyond this, all you have to know is how to knit (but hardly how to purl), how to decrease, how to increase, how to weave, and how to keep as cool in the presence of markers as a Mississippi pilot.

Try to acquire the habit of using safety-pins as markers; they don't interfere as much as do ring-markers, which have to be passed from needle to needle every time you come to them. Safety-pins may be pinned between stitches, or even right in the stitches themselves, and serve to show you *which* stitch swallows *which* stitch (or gives birth to which stitch, as the case may be), and gently and gradually cause you to consider exactly *what* you are doing, and *why*—valuable steps towards becoming your own designer. I often leave my safety-pins far behind me in my knitting, but not so far that my left thumb no longer feels them, to be reminded that it's time to increase, or decrease, or whistle up my brain for a little activity.

PITHY DIRECTIONS:
OPEN-COLLARED SHIRT WITH
GARTER STITCH TRIM AND PLACKET-NECK

GAUGE: 5 sts to 1″. Width around: 40″.

MATERIALS: 3 4 oz skeins 1-ply "Homespun". 4 (4 oz) skeins knitting worsted, or any yarn which knits up at the above GAUGE. 1 16″, 1 24″ circular needle of a size to give *you* correct GAUGE. (Approx size 4–8).

BORDER: Cast on 10 sts and work firmly in garter-st (all knit, back-and-forth.) Make I-Cord edge (see appendix) on one side as follows: *K to within 3 sts of end, wool fwd, sl 3 sts as if to P. K 1 row. Rep from * until there are 200 ridges of garter-stitch. Join end to beginning.

BODY: Knit up 1 st in each of the 200 ridges of border with 24″ needle. Work for 17″, or desired length to underarm. Put 16 sts (8% of 200) on pieces of wool at underarms, having 84 sts on back and on front.

SLEEVES: Make 60-ridge border as for body. Join, and knit up 60 sts around with 16″ circular needle. Continue around, increasing 2 sts at underarm every 5th rnd to 66 sts (33% of 200). At $5\frac{1}{2}$″ or desired length, place 16 sts at underarm on piece of wool.

Unite all 268 sts of body and sleeves on 24″ needle, matching underarms. K 2 rnds.

PLACKET: Place marker at center-front between sts 42 and 43. K to within 5 sts of marker, Cast on 10. Turn, and from now on work back-and-forth. *K 10, P to last 10 sts, K 7, wool fwd, sl 3 as if to P. Turn. K to last 3 sts, wool fwd, sl 3 as if to P. Turn. Rep from * until further notice.

RAGLAN SHAPING starts 1″ after union of body and sleeves. Place 4 markers, one each in first and last sts of front and of back. Decrease 2 sts at each of these 4 points every second row. At the same time, place. . . .

BUTTONHOLES: The first one (see Appendix) is placed after 5 ridges of garter-stitch, and two more after 10 & 20 ridges.

When all sleeve-sts are decreased away, cast off 5 sts at right-hand neck-edge, thus:—*K 2, SSK, replace sts on left-hand needle. Repeat 4 more times. Work to left-hand end and repeat from *.

COLLAR: Work back-and-forth in garter-stitch on remaining 68 sts, continuing I-C border. Inc. 1 st after I-C edge at beg of each row by M 1. At $3\frac{1}{2}''$ work I-C casting-off as above. Put in Phoney Seams if desired. Weave under-arms. Catch down lower section of placket.

OPEN-COLLARED SHIRT FROM THE TOP DOWN. FACED COLLAR AND NECK-OPENING.

GAUGE: 6 sts to 1″. Width: 40″ around.

MATERIALS: 10oz Shetland wool, or any yarn which knits up at 6 sts to 1″. 1 16″, 1 24″ circular needle of a size to give *you* correct GAUGE (Approx size 2–5)

Cast on 204 sts for collar-edge. Join, and K 2 rnds. Decr 2 sts at beginning and at half-way point every 2nd rnd until 160 sts remain. Cast off 40 sts at center of one side, and continue around. Mark center 40 sts of other side and mark 2 sts at each end of these 40 sts with 1 st in between the 2. Inc 1 st each side of the 4 marked sts every 2nd for raglan-shaping.

When there are 60 sleeve-sts between the raglans, place them on 2 pieces of wool. Also place the center-front 40 sts on a piece of wool. Continue around on body-sts, casting on 20 sts at each underarm. Work on 240 sts for desired length for body. If desired, work short rows and lower-back shaping as in text. At 17″, or desired length, make hem.

For sleeves knit up 80 sts and work to desired length, decreasing 2 sts at underarm every 1″. Make hems at lower edges. Machine-stitch and cut facing at center-front. Pick up the stitches at lower edge of facing and work about $3\frac{1}{2}''$.

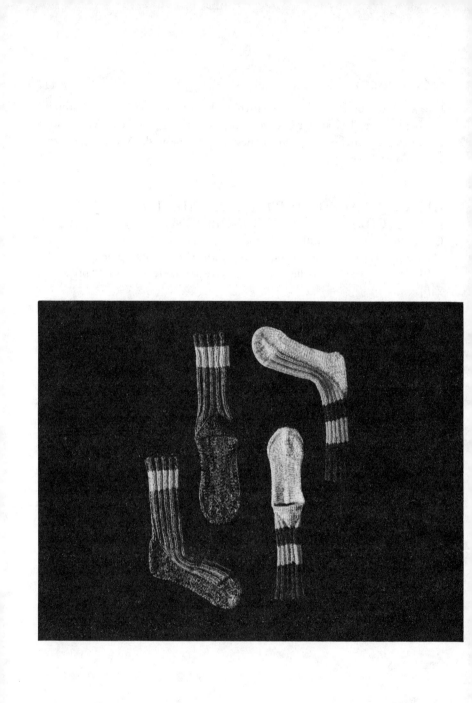

NOVEMBER

Moccasin Socks

PLANS FOR THIS CHAPTER have been scrapped in favor of describing the project on which I am currently and most actively engaged. I can think of little else.

The item, hot from the griddle, which I now unveil is the Moccasin Sock; the Breakthrough Sock, the Not-To-Be-Ground-Down Sock; the Eventually Totally Re-footable Sock. Call it what you will; all the above tentative titles apply.

If you are a maker and mender of socks you have shared with me the heart-break of finding holes right next to the places which have been carefully strengthened with nylon. Many of the offending holes are right under the heel, just past the point where the heel-turning was completed and knitting was continued around, minus nylon. To have carried it further would have resulted in an ugly stripe around the entire instep, so this idea was abandoned. One could have knitted in some nylon just at this point for an inch or so, joining it in and cutting it for each round, but, in the argot of my youth "What a swot." Besides, I refuse to countenance a new design which is not practicable for and encouraging to my buddy, the average knitter, and I wouldn't dream of fussing her with such a chore.

As you will remember from the August chapter, I tackled this problem with a measure of success while camping this summer. However when I next reviewed the mending-basket my irritation was aggravated anew by socks with holes under the *ball* of the foot, at a spot where I, in my wisdom, had decided that it was much too soon to have started incorporating the toe-nylon. Clearly, more research was in order; one should be able to strengthen the whole sole, but without involving the upper part of the foot.

I was sitting in the car on the long trip home from a little grandchild-doting, and my main project had run out of wool. Luckily I had some of the splendid Dinkum wool from Australia with me. I started doodling and thinking of grandchildren at the same time: at least this is the only explanation for the sudden explosion of an idea. . . . .

What's wrong with baby-booties?

Baby booties fit the foot competently, and the sole is made last, so that it can easily and functionally include nylon. An inch or so of the side of the foot can include nylon too.

Yes; you say, but what about heel-strengthening? Your bootie-sole won't come high enough.

Into my mental processes at this point I will not go, because, to my regret, I can no longer recall them. This is one of the few, but intense, drawbacks to old age; one forgets.

In many cases forgetting seems to be a protective mechanism. The brain has slowed down and no longer has the capacity to retain irrelevant detail. Was it Thursday or Friday of the week before last that the Old Man saw those three otters in the river, and they weren't afraid of him a bit, except for their initial huffing and blowing, but went right on gambolling downstream, leaving him to fish, and the moment one of them climbed on a log with a small carp in its mouth the Old Man got his first and only bite, a nice Northern?

My stars, *his* memory is far from enfeebled. Each detail is preserved as clearly as when it happened, and who cares what day of the week it was?

Where did I put the little blue egg-boiling pot? The brain refuses to cooperate. Never mind; use something else; the pot will turn up. Sure enough, it did. Adhering to the belief that boiled-egg water is good for houseplants, I had taken the pot to the bedroom windowsill where I am encouraging last winter's cyclamen. I found it next time I watered. Smart brain; it knew I'd find the pot eventually, and saved its waning but still valuable powers for composing a letter to a desperate knitter who had miscalculated his neck-stitches.

Solution of the heel-strengthening problem could have been *inspiration,* but I doubt it; I am not the inspiration-prone type. I gnaw on problems, knitting and ripping and knitting and ripping. The project sometimes improves and sometimes worsens. I think this is called empiricism, and I enjoy its practice inordinately.

In any case, skimming and joggling and skimming through New York State, Pennsylvania, and Ohio respectively, I came up with the Pointed Heel, and now I can lay the Moccasin Sock before you:

First make the leg, back-and-forth, in K 2, P 2, rib, on, for the sake of argument, 44 sts, with a single knitted stitch at either end on the right side, to make the back seam more satisfactory. When you are at a point $1\frac{1}{2}''$ above the heel of the shoe, leave three stitches on a piece of wool or safety-pin at each end, and start the instep-shaping. This is done by decreasing one stitch each end, every second row, until you have half as many stitches as you started with (22). I like to decrease on the right side: K 1, SSK, work to last three stitches, K 2 together, K 1. On the wrong side work the stitches as they present themselves.

Now it is time to advise you most strongly to slip the first stitch of every row in this whole project, and this goes for the short rows you will be making later. Opinions vary on first stitches—some knitters work them; some slip them. I am a congenital slipper, but the main thing, as I see it, is to be consistent. Be all this as it may, in *this* sock every first stitch should be slipped (as if to knit, or as if to purl, depending on how it lies), or there may be trouble when the time comes to knit up the foot-stitches.

When the instep-shaping is finished, work straight in ribbing until you are 8″ from the place where the three stitches were left on safety-pins. *Join in nylon thread* and work 1″ (less for shorter socks; more for longer ones) in stocking-stitch.

The toe is now shaped in a rather unusual manner:

Divide the stitches roughly into thirds. For instance, if there are 22 stitches, take 8 for the center-section and 7 for each side. If there are 26 stitches, take 8 for the center-section and 9 for each side. Or 10 for the center-section and 8 for each side; it doesn't matter much; knitting is not always that exact a science.

The center section is going to consume the side sections at the rate of two stitches every second row, on the knit side, as follows:

*Knit to within one stitch of the center section, knit two together, knit to last stitch of center section, SSK, complete row, and purl back. Repeat from * and continue to decrease in this way until only the center section remains, ending with a knit row.

Place the remaining stitches on the 16″ circular needle, knit up one stitch in each of the loops at the lefthand side of the instep, knit up the six stitches waiting on safety-pins at the heel-back and so on down the other side of the instep. All stitches are now on the circular needle, and work continues around. The number of stitches is very roughly double that originally cast on, depending on the length of the foot. The thing is beginning to shape up. As you will see, the toe-shaping curls right over the toes and down under them.

The next step is the shaping of a good and elegantly-pointed heel. When, on the first round, you come to those six safety-pin stitches, knit them, and then turn. Purl back for seven stitches, slipping the first one as if to purl, the way I told you. Turn, slip one, knit seven. Turn, slip one, purl eight, and so on, taking up one more stitch at the end of each short row. When you have half the stitches you originally cast on (22), the heel is shaped. The time has come for the bootie-foot; not a true bootie-foot, as the toe is already shaped, actually more of a bewitching moccasin-foot.

Knit around mindlessly for 1″, and then decrease sharply along the toe section, that is, start knitting two together where the ribbing stops, and stop where the ribbing starts again. I assure you that during knitting this makes sense, and will cause you to knit two together about sixteen times. Work half an inch, and repeat the decreasing, on half the number of stitches, naturally. Both these groups of increasings should be centered, so that they will pull in the toe properly. You may work the second decreasing at the heel too, if you wish.

When the piece of stocking-stitch is two inches high (or should I say deep?), or a little more for a thick foot, the knitting is finished. Cut wool and nylon, leaving a piece about 24″ long. Draw the toe-stitches together, fasten them securely, and weave the two sides together. Draw together the same number of stitches for the heel as you did for the toe, and finish off. There will be a small swelling under the ball of the foot, but this is easily steam-ironed away, never to be seen again.

Now examine what you have wrought: I hope you will agree that this is a stylish sock, the like of which you have not seen before. I think the pointed heel looks better than the usual square one, and it is more functional. It comes up nicely beyond the point where the shoe-heel chews into the sock, and makes a graceful slope. If your sock-wearer tends to favor brown shoes, you can make the sole in matching brown wool, irrespective of the color of the rest of the sock, and the same goes for the chronic wearer of black shoes. In the case of a woodsman's sock, where the entire foot is concealed in the boot, make the top in a light color if you wish, but use something practical for the sole; you know how hard it is to get the feet of pale socks really clean-looking, no matter how pure they are in fact.

To tell the truth, I'm rather proud of the toe; it curls over at the end in such a cosy and protective manner, and it adapts so well to feet of different lengths; its arabesque-like shaping will be the admiration of all when it is wiggled in front of a good open fire. Don't think it sprang fully-armed from my brain; if I made one trial toe I must have made fifteen or twenty, ripping ruthlessly between each; you have no idea how many ways there are to shape a toe. I rather wish I had kept a record of them—my little stunted attempts. Never mind; they are safely stowed away in the subconscious, to emerge one day perhaps in the form of a shoulder or a bonnet. . .

The moccasin-foot is childishly easy to replace when it finally wears out. One of the saddest sights in knitting is a pair of whited sepulchre socks, in perfect shape as far as the eye can see, but a hodgepodge of laborious darning below the shoeline, each darn making it more valuable in the darner's eye, and more difficult to jettison. When further darning is out of the question, the only recourse is to divide the sock at the ankle, and make a new foot from there on down, thereby condemning a pair of perfectly good sock-legs to unmatching feet, and the lowly status of work-socks. With the Eventually Totally Re-footable Sock the sole and heel and toe can be replaced without disturbing the instep, and nobody a penny the wiser.

Let us not think too far ahead, however; replacement need not happen for years with nylon in the sole. Yes, I know; nylon isn't always too easy to find. If I can't find those small cards of Heel'N'Toe, I use fine half-and-half wool and nylon. A whole ball of this sounds like a great capital expenditure, but it will last for many socks, and, if in a neutral shade, will blend with many colors. I have also used heavy polyester Dual Duty thread; one spool will strengthen one foot.

The Old Man has made the noble offer of some of his nylon fishline. I have used this only once, and recently, so can give no data on its lasting qualities. Naturally he donates it only when its tensile strength is presumably unequal to playing the big one.

The moccasin Sock has several fringe-benefits:

Firstly, as I have already said, it can be re-footed with ease and success.

Secondly, it will use up odd amounts of wool which are not sufficient for a whole pair of socks. After leg and instep are finished you may feel free to change colors. You may also change colors after the triangular heel-section is done if you are persnicketty about the heel showing in a different color.

Thirdly (a), you are working on a brand-new design, which is always interesting, and (b), you will amaze your friends.

Fourthly, and this applies to all designs in this book: why not? Valid reasons for *not* using any of my funny ways of knitting will be welcomed by me with open arms, so that I can set about improvements.

A FEW WORDS ON PURLING, on which I want to make my position clear. The avoidance of purling where possible has given me the reputation of hating it, which is not strictly true.

Purling has its place, and a useful one. Without it, many beautiful stitch-patterns would be impossible. Without it, what could be used for the background in Aran patterns? Without it, how could one make that marvellously neat edge for garter-stitch by casting off, in purl, on the right side?

However, for many people purling is slower than knitting, and for those of us who work with the wool over the left forefinger it may be positively awkward.

Scratch any knitter, and the odds are that you will find that he or she admits to a preference for the knit row, when working back-and-forth in stocking-stitch. One is happy to go to the trouble of purling, no matter how one performs it, when it has a function, and a pretty and visible effect, but why purl if you don't have to?

As one who does not enjoy work only for its results, but also for the pleasure it produces in itself, I set about the elimination of purling when and where possible, and came up quite easily with the solution of working round and round on four needles, or, better, on a circular needle, so that stocking-stitch could be produced without the necessity of purling back.

When working lace-patterns, one is frequently required to "purl back on alternate rows". Why not knit around instead of purling back? Why not indeed.

When working Aran patterns for fisherman sweaters one does not, of course, purl back; one *works* back, knitting the knit stitches and purling the purl ones, depending on how they lie. Sometimes, when there is a cable or a travelling-stitch on the right side, it is not too clear which are the knit stitches and which the purl ones on the wrong side, and one has to peer over the top of the needle to make sure. If one were working round and round on the right side, this would not be necessary. I think you will be surprised at how automatic and pleasant circular Aran-knitting becomes after the first few inches. The eye and the hand take over, and the brain is free to wander. Or to remain blank, perhaps, and re-charge its depleted batteries. After all, do we have to think *all* the time?

NOVEMBER NOTES, ANYONE?

In some quarters November is considered rather a dull month, but not at our house. It is a time of snugging down; of finding, and foiling, sources of draughts; of augmenting the woodpile, putting up the bird-feeders, starting in on some serious reading, and knitting—always knitting. One plans and executes the remaining knitted Christmas presents, and considers some ambitious project for that distant snowlocked time of After Christmas. One is assailed, nay, bowled over, by sudden flashes of inspiration, as it might be by a moccasin-sock. Did I say I am never inspired? Pay no attention to me; I'll say anything. Inspiration is unsettling to a degree. If not pinned down immediately by being worked on—actually knitted up—it melts away like morning dew and is lost forever. Even after being knitted up it tends to be forgotten again. My proof of this is a large plastic bag I own, stuffed with odd wools and becalmed projects. If I ever find myself sans knitting ideas, I'll rummage in that bag and resurrect one.

At least the Moccasin-Sock is pinned down, knitted, and described. Perhaps you'd like to try a pair? Here are directions, on 60 stitches for the blind follower. The thinking knitter can glean two different pairs from one chapter.

PITHY DIRECTIONS:
MOCCASIN SOCK.

GAUGE: 6 sts to 1″.

SIZE: Average adult.

MATERIALS: About 3 oz fine sock wool suitable for above GAUGE. 1 pr needles and 1 16″ circular needle of a size to give correct GAUGE (about #0–#3). Nylon thread.

Cast on, with straight needles, 60 sts. Slip all first sts throughout the sock.

Row 1, P 1, *K 2, P 2, rep from *, ending P 1.

Row 2. K 1, *P 2, K 2, rep from *, ending K 1. Rep these 2 rows for 8″ or desired length for leg.

Place 3 sts at either end on pieces of wool or safety-pins. 54 sts remain, with K 2 at either end on the right side. *On right side, sl 1, SSK, work to within 3 sts of end, K 2 tog, K 1. Work back. Rep from * until 30 sts remain.

Work straight until piece measures 8″ from sts on safety-pins. *Join nylon* and work 1″ in stocking-st for 10″ sock (2″ for 11″ sock, 0″ for 9″ sock). Shape toe, starting on right side:

K 9, K 2 tog, K 8, SSK, K 9. Purl back.

K 8, K 2 tog, K 8, SSK, K 8. Purl back.

K 7, K 2 tog, K 8, SSK, K 7. Purl back, and so on until on the last row, on the right side, 10 sts remain. Put them on the 16″ circular needle.

Working from the right side, knit up about 53 sts along lefthand side of instep, knit 6 sts from safety-pins, as well as sts from righthand side of instep. Work around to safety-pin sts. Knit them, turn. P 7, turn. K 8, turn. P 9, turn, and so on, until you have purled 29 sts and turned. Work around on all sts for 1″. Next rnd decrease for toe by K 2 tog 20 times at this point. Work $\frac{1}{2}$″ and K 2 tog 10 times (half as many times) at toe and at heel. When circular piece is 2″ long draw tog 10 sts at toe, weave sides tog, and draw tog 10 sts at heel.

Sew back-seam neatly, "weaving" from the right side, if you are fussy.

In the unlikely event that these socks wear out, unravel the feet and refresh the little pets with new ones, to double their lifespan.

DECEMBER

Hurry-up Last-Minute Sweater

ADD UNTO CHRISTMAS WITH DISCRETION; delete at your peril.

Is an exciting new improved Christmas every year really necessary? Is it in the spirit of the Solstice? The human heart hankers after stability and tradition. The feeling and atmosphere of Christmases past, the anticipation of those to come, and the magic presence of Christmas now should all blend and blur, to give the distraught soul something to hang on to in a year bedevilled by new improved machines, soaps, music, spectator sports and recipes, many of which will prove to be dull, destructive, and sometimes downright damnable. Let us try to keep at least Christmas the way it has been for generations, and infiltrate novelty delicately and with caution. As a good start why not try to abide by the comforting tradition of handmade and homemade presents?

Do you have hanging over you something that you well intended to make, but which you have never got around to starting, even? You do? A sweater? So do I.

Embarking on a sweater at this late date smacks of madness, but it can be done, and done without using up too much of your precious December-time. The main thing is to make it very thick. The thicker the knitting, the fewer the stitches; the fewer the stitches, the sooner finished, right? Not finished as soon as mathematics would tell you—the fingers are not quite as agile with thick wool as with thin—but still, finished with surprising speed.

At $2\frac{1}{2}$ stitches to $1''$ you can make a $40''$ sweater on only 100 stitches, with proportionately few rounds. An extra 5 stitches will bring it up to a $42''$ sweater, and so on, up or down. Get out some great fat circular needles—a $16''$ and a $24''$ one—and some Sheepsdown, and start on a swatch. If the hurry is enormous, and you are pretty sure of your GAUGE, you can even start on a sleeve—$\frac{1}{5}$ of 100: 20 stitches for the cuff—and use *it* as your swatch. If it comes out a *little* too big or a *little* too small (the former can be pulled in with a tightish hem; the latter will stretch if it has to), you can adjust the number of stitches for the upper sleeve and the body.

I have set aside eight 4oz. skeins of Sheepsdown and am using a #$10\frac{1}{2}$ needle for the simple reason that this is the largest size in which there exists a $16''$ circular needle for the sleeves. With a size $10\frac{1}{2}$ I can attain a GAUGE of $2\frac{1}{2}$ stitches to $1''$ with this wool. If you can NOT, take a larger $24''$ needle for the body, and make the sleeves on four needles. This sweater really must be made in the round—it is designed for it, and, besides, think of the time you will save by not having to sew it up.

I call it the "Wishbone" Sweater, and this is its first introduction to knitters. Do *not* try it at a smaller GAUGE with finer wool. I have, and for some reason it doesn't work, which is a mystery to me. I tried it at a GAUGE of 4 stitches to $1''$, knitted and ripped the shoulders five times, finally gave up in despair, and ended with a rather complicated modification of a wishbone. Why the relationship of stitch gauge and row gauge should vary between thick and less-thick wool is so far an enigma to me, but one that I hope to solve one day, given a long life and good knitting physiology.

I shall make my sweater quite large—firstly because it is for a large person, and secondly because very thick sweaters should measure at least one inch, if not two inches, larger than you would think, as the thickness of their fabric makes them smaller inside than out. If you don't believe this, envision making a garment out of a foam-rubber mattress, and think how much wider the circumference would be than the inside measurement. The same applies to a thick sweater. Mine will be $46''$ around *outside*, which means 115 stitches at a GAUGE of $2\frac{1}{2}$ stitches to $1''$. I shall bring this up to 116 stitches for the convenience of being able to divide by two: 57 stitches for the front, 57 for the back, plus a seam-stitch on either side.

I shall start with but 110 stitches, however. Of these 110 I shall allow only 51 for the back, and shall work straight for about $3\frac{1}{2}''$, keeping safety-pins in the seam-stitches, but otherwise paying no attention to them for the time being.

At $3\frac{1}{2}''$ I shall increase the remaining 6 stitches, evenly-spaced, across the 51 stitches of the back, as described on page 106: work seam-stitch, K 3, M 1, (K 9, M 1) 5 times, K 3, work seam-stitch. This gives a sneaky piece of shaping to the lower back, and counteracts the lamentable tendency of all sweaters—handknitted and machine-made—to widen at the shoulder and hang loose at the lower back. Machines may not care to cope with this problem, but we are handknitters, and not so hidebound.

An additional way to give a better fit to the back of a sweater is by the use of Short Rows (see Appendix). These are worked, back-and-forth, fairly regularly-spaced, across the back only, two or three times as you proceed from hem to underarm. At the large GAUGE at which we are working, each pair of short rows will give an extra $\frac{1}{2}''$ of length where it is most needed. Length to the underarm is up to you. I still like my sweaters $26''$–$27''$ long, but I observe those of others slyly creeping up to a marked shortness. Suit yourself.

Now start the sleeves, if you haven't already done this in the form of a swatch. I cast on 24 stitches (20% of 116, approx.), and increased 2 stitches at the underarm every 4th round. Three stitches were kept between the increases, to facilitate the dropping of the seam-stitch when the time came, and I increased by "Make 1", i.e. a firm backward loop over the right-hand needle. If you are one who loves perfection, twist the loop one way for the right-hand increase, and the other way for the left-hand increase. Few will notice this, but it will give you an inner glow.

For the Wishbone Sweater the upper arm is 40% of the body-width, or 46 stitches for a 116-stitch sweater, so continue with the paired increases until you have this many; then work straight.

As soon as body and sleeves are the length to the underarm that you want them to be (my body is $19\frac{1}{2}''$ and my sleeves $17''$), you may put in phoney seams. (see Appendix). Then it is time to join the three pieces on the $24''$

needle, and work the really exciting and brand-new yoke. It was unvented this summer, after many trials and rippings, and I repeat, *Don't* try it in finer wool at a smaller GAUGE unless you want utter frustration.

Put 9 stitches (8% of 116) on pieces of wool at the underarms on body and on sleeves. Very convenient; the seam-stitch can be stitch number 5. (Yes; I know that 8% of 116 is 9.28, but who ever heard of .28 of a stitch? Are we mathematicians or knitters? Percentages are our servants; not we theirs.) When all the remaining stitches are on the 24″ needle, they should amount to exactly 172.

The sleeves, which now have 37 stitches each, are going to lap over the body at the rate of one stitch every second round, so carefully mark the first and last stitches of either sleeve with small safety-pins. Work one round plain, and start decreasing on the second round:

*Work across Front to within 1 stitch of the first marked stitch, K 2 together. Work across sleeve to second marked stitch, slip it, knit the next body-stitch, and pass the slipped stitch over (or, better, SSK). Repeat from * across Back, and complete the round. You have decreased 4 stitches in all. Work one round plain.

Repeat these two rounds, from the first *, and you will find that the sleeves are starting to creep over the body. But not fast enough, you will say, and you are right.

When the total of back- and front-stitches equals (within 1 stitch actually) the 37 stitches of each sleeve—19 each for back and front—it is time to go into the second stage of decreasing.

Mark 3 stitches at the center of each sleeve, and decrease 2 stitches at these points every second round: work to within 1 stitch of the three marked stitches, K 2 together, K 1, SSK. Do this on each shoulder every other round, and you will double the general rate of decrease and make good functional-looking shoulders. Continue the shoulder-decreasings until 23 sleeve-stitches remain on either side ($\frac{1}{5}$ of the 116 stitches originally cast on). Then stop the shoulder-decreasings, but continue with the front- and back-decreasings. By the time they meet at center-front and center-back the total number of stitches will be just right for the neck—around 46, or 40% of the original 116 body-stitches.

If you have many more or less than this something must have gone awry—better check—but don't break your heart over 3 or 4 stitches.

All decreasing now stops, and the back-of-neck shaping is worked. *Do not omit this:* it is vital to the fit and good looks of any sweater; with this heavy wool it will consist of only three short rows:

At left shoulder, turn, P 23 stitches (or about half), turn, K 25 stitches, turn, P 27 stitches, turn. That's all. Continue around for 5 rounds. Cast off by the casting-on method (see Appendix). This is a little more trouble, but worth it. It is elastic, looks superb and ropelike, and may well deceive other knitters into thinking that this sweater was made from the top. If you prefer you may purl one round to turn the neck-hem, and finish as given below.

Weave underarms, and the sweater is done except for the hems. Don't fuss because the phoney seamlines fail to meet by half a stitch; nothing can be done about this.

Hems are made in finer wool—perhaps knitting worsted weight, or even finer, and may be of a different color. Strive for an approximate GAUGE of 5 stitches to 1″. Naturally, at this GAUGE you will need more stitches for the hems than for the corresponding sections of the sweater, and the right proportion is achieved by knitting up two stitches at the back of the casting-on (or, in the case of the deceptive neck, of the casting-off stitches), and then making 1 stitch, around. (*Knit up 2, M 1, repeat from * around). Hems for cuffs and lower edge may be about 12 rounds deep. For the neck, work about 8 rounds, then K 2, M 1, around, and work a further 8 rounds before sewing the hem down, lightly and elastically, without casting off. The last increase-round causes it to lie smoothly under the slightly stand-up collar.

Now isn't that a sweater to astonish the weak nerves of all beholders? Mine took eight 4 oz skeins to the last fraction of an ounce. As I can knit up one skein in one hour, I reckon that the whole job takes only 30 minutes a day between December 1st and December 16th. This much time even the busiest person can afford, sandwiched between cookies, card-writing, loathesome last-minute shopping-trips, present-wrapping, carol-singing, and decking the halls with boughs of holly.

PITHY DIRECTIONS
FOR WISHBONE SWEATER.

GAUGE: 10 sts to 4″ (2½ sts to 1″). Width around 46″ (outside). For each 2″ more or less wanted, add or subtract 5 sts and follow percentages.

MATERIALS: 8–9 skeins Sheepsdown. 1 16″, 1 24″ circular needle of a size to give *you* above GAUGE.

Cast on 110 sts (116 less 6) on 24″ needle. Join and work around for 3½″. Inc. 6 sts evenly-spaced across back. When body is 19½″ long, or wanted length, put 9 sts (8% of 116) on pieces of wool at underarms.

SLEEVES: With 16″ needle or 4 needles cast on 24 sts (20% of 116). Join, and work around, increasing 2 sts at underarm every 4th rnd. At 46 sts (40% of 116), work straight to underarm (about 18″). Put 9 sts at underarm on piece of wool. Place all sts on 24″ needle, matching underarms, and work around, decreasing 4 sts every 2nd rnd, 1 at each end of sleeve-sts (see text).

When back and front-sts combined equal 37 sts of sleeve, decr 2 sts at center of sleeves every 2nd rnd until 23 sts remain (20% of 116). Continue around, decreasing at front and back only, until these decreasings meet.

SHAPE NECK-BACK: Starting at L shoulder, turn, P 23 to R shoulder, turn, K 25, turn, P 27. Work 5 rnds and cast off. Put hems at neck, cuffs, and lower edge (see text). Weave underarms.

WERE YOU EVER SNOWED IN?

For years it has been my Heart's Desire, and this year it has come to pass. In the afternoon it started to snow, finely and with determination. Just before supper the plough came through, with the boys on board, shouting Happy New Year. After supper I gave myself a treat and went out and shovelled a small path to the garage, to save work in the morning, but so did it snow and blow through the night that by morning not a trace of my path remained, nor any sign of the road-ploughing of the evening before.

The first job was to clear paths; then the Old Man plunged out to the blue jay feeder. He has been training his large flock of blue jays not to infringe on the rights of smaller birds at the feeder near the window. The jays have been so good at sticking to their humble cracked corn over near the woods while chickadees and woodpeckers feast on suet and sunflower seeds at the house that it would never do to give them ideas. They were all perched patiently and decoratively on their popple-tree, and he just made it, in his hipboots, bearing a bucketful of corn.

Breakfast followed, for them and for us, and then we went up to shovel the snow off the large flattish roof of the New Bit. We started where it was about a foot deep, and progressed laboriously to where it had drifted to over 30″. From time to time the roof gave a faint groan and a sigh of relief as its load lightened, and in an hour we were done.

The Old Man then put on his snowshoes to forge his way to the highroad and see how things looked (one lane open but no noticeable traffic), while I made the beguiling discovery that the snow around the house was of just the right consistency to be cut with a shovel and lifted in large, light, shovel-sized chunks. In no time at all I had the beginnings of a fine igloo, the roof of which, however, finally defeated me. It's much more diverting to remove snow with a constructive purpose in mind, and it seemed that the work went faster, though doubtless this was an enjoyable delusion.

My kind of character enjoys work best when work is fun, and progress can be noted and gloated over. When I have a long plain piece of knitting ahead I put a safety-pin at each day's beginning to show me how I am coming. When working in the dark—for instance in the car on the long trip home—I knit one stitch with the wool the wrong way round the needle if I can't find a safety-pin. When I come to this spot again my right-hand needle is startled by the twisted stitch. I work into it from the back, of course, to keep it straight, but again wrap the wool the wrong way round the needle, and repeat this for the next stitch, so that when I next come to this point there are two twisted stitches. Aha! two rounds already. The first one is twisted again, the second worked normally, and the third one twisted. And so on with the fourth and fifth rounds; every time I come to my twisted stitches I know how many rounds have been accomplished. How loony can you get? I know; but this is the way the minds of some of us work, and why not give your mind its head if nobody is hurt thereby? Naturally when conversation takes root, buds, and blossoms, these tricks fall into abeyance, and knitting goes on automatically. But in a good well-worn marriage long silences are as frequent as good argle-bargles, and as enjoyable. I imagine that many of us can look back to some early pang of apprehension: what in hell shall we TALK about in all the loving, cherishing years ahead? What a bootless fear! In any case try to arrange your knitting so that you are never without some soothing piece of plain work which just ticks along, sans brain or eye.

What? You can't knit in the dark? Stuff and nonsense; anybody can. Shut your eyes. Knit one stitch. Open your eyes and look at the stitch; it's all right. Shut your eyes and knit two stitches. Open them. Shut them. Knit three stitches. Falling off a log is no comparison. If, when your eyes are shut, your left thumb or right needle sends you a message that it is up against something funny, it probably is—be it a twisted or dropped stitch, or the fact that the stitch of the row below has been worked into. Rectify it, and shut your eyes again. If you are in the car in the dark, hold your knitting up against the light of your headlights on the road and fix matters. For the faint of heart it may be better to wait until somebody comes up from behind, and you can use *his* headlights. If your driver, noticing your struggles, offers to turn on the inside light for a moment, you are in luck, and have allied yourself to an A number one spouse.

All that shovelling is telling on a sedentary old knitter; I feel a nap coming on. I shall take my knitting and a horizontal position, and let the gentle suggestion of the latter slowly take precedence over the former.

THE DECEMBER CHAPTER is filling up fast; room must be made for one more useful trick. Directions in knitting "books" are fine, but their writers have little space to tell you of the small dodges that make all the difference. If you frequent a good knit shop or wool department, where there is a competent and kind instructress, she may, if not bedevilled by too many beginners or obliged to ring up sales in the intervals of helping, be able to give you many useful tips. But if you live in a knitting vacuum or have had small opportunity to learn the tricks of the trade, the following may be welcome:

You have cast off a cuff, or a neckline, or even the bottom of a circular sweater made from the neck down, and have a thread left for finishing off. *Don't* pull it tight. With a blunt sewing-needle, thread it delicately through the very first stitch of the casting-off, and then back through the last stitch whence it came. Adjust the tension, and finish it off. You have united the cast-off stitches indetectably, and achieved another of those small satisfactions which contribute to a contented life.

Time and space for just one more; do you know how to take off a few inches from a completed garment? People have been known to take them off brutally, with scissors; let us avert our eyes from such a practice. It is nigh on to humanly impossible to cut straight along a given row without slipping with the scissors up or down into neighboring rows. That means three rows lost, added to which there is the nuisance of dealing with numberless small crescents of wool resulting from the actual cutting. It will be some time and many damns later that you achieve the desired result of a row of stitches on the needle again.

The best way is to snip just one stitch, which leaves two cut ends, and to unravel them in an easterly and a westerly direction until they meet again on the other side. How poetic. On a large piece of knitting these ends will become inconveniently long, and it is perfectly permissible to cut them short from time to time unless you are as thrifty with wool as I am. There you are, then, with a neat round of stitches to pick up and cast off. Or to continue knitting on, as the case may be.

At the risk of repeating myself interminably, I must warn you that you can only knit *down*—that is, in the opposite direction to that of the original work—*if* your fabric is stocking-stitch or garter-stitch. Any stitch-pattern or even color-pattern will be half a stitch off if worked downwards when the original garment was worked upwards.

The reason is logical, but hard to make clear.

Knitting is formed by a series of loops pulled through loops pulled through loops to the end of time or to "desired length". By picking up loops and working in the opposite direction you are really picking up the concavities *between* loops, and it is sheer unexpected witchcraft that stocking-stitch and garter-stitch will permit such an anomaly. Be grateful for this and don't expect any more.

The stove murmurs to itself, the kettle sings, the cats purr in a patch of sun, the clock ticks away the year. . . .

Envoi.

You and I have swung one another, and our knitting, around and through the seasons. Now Christmas Eve, Christmas Day, even Boxing Day, are behind us. The year is running down.

These few days between Christmas and the New Year are for holding the breath, for sitting still and observing, for summoning energies against the future. There is a hush, unbroken even by the click of knitting-needles, although perhaps by the turning of the pages of the beautiful new Christmas books. The house still shines from its pre-holiday scrubbing, meals are simple—there is a power of gnawing on a big turkey and sweetmeats abound—and we are snowed in.

Soon the tree will come down, and the ornaments be put away for another year. To me this is one of the most touching of the annual rites; much more so than that of putting up the tree when all is festivity and excitement. Where shall we all be when these boxes are opened again? What is about to befall? What joys are in store? We are thankful for the past year, and hold a good thought over the next.

The small battered tree-baubles—mementos of how many years, remaining members of how many sets—may now spend fifty weeks under the garage-rafters, at the mercy of wax-melting heat and enterprising mice, until their High Season returns.

The manger, with its precious German waxen Holy Family, shepherd, donkey, and hornless cow; its eight Holy Three Kings, picked up at Woolworths over the years because they were irresistible; its two china snow-babies who sledded and rolled down the icing of my childhood's Christmas cakes, and the rest of its heterogeneous inhabitants, is dismantled. It was made from scrap-lumber and an orange-crate for our first American Christmas, thirty-six years ago. The roof lifts off, the sides pull out, and it folds flat—this in preparation for the many moves we knew we would be making. As it turned out, we made only five, well below the national average, but who could foresee that?

If I had known then what I now know about the United States I would have greeted that Statue of Liberty with glad cries that bleak November day in 1937, instead of with rather apprehensive gloom.

My ideas of this country had been gathered from her travelling citizens, from the movies, and from "Babbitt." (A ray of light was provided by my having been brought up on "Little Women".) I was convinced that we should live in a shabby brownstone walkup with four families to share the facilities; that we should spend our summers panting on the front steps, or walking along something called a boardwalk eating popcorn and cotton candy, and our vacations in a landscape strongly resembling the Jersey Flats. I knew we could never aspire to Cadillacs, to estates on Long Island, and the cool Adirondacks in summer.

That there was a spacious and hospitable, a warm and friendly middleland between these extremes, with lovely landscape and good neighbors, somehow escaped me. I must pinch myself occasionally, and remind myself that I am actually at home in the United States, and am a genuine adult—or shall we say elderly?—citizen of this country. To each his own nationality, but how fortunate are we to be able to live where we really want to live.

I RECONNOITERED IN MY WOOL-ROOM YESTERDAY; it is full of possibilities for the New Year. Another Aran perhaps, to start off with? Should it blow tradition and be hooded? Six pairs of socks for the Old Man? His "Woodsman's Sock" shelf is groaning, but the ranks of the lighter socks are thinning. Cushioncovers? What a chance for experiment with color-patterns and Aran curlicues. A shawl with a ten-inch lace border, and perhaps design the border myself? I never did design a lace-pattern. A huge afghan to keep one's knees warm while being knitted? A lace-edging for a valance, why not? A revolutionary pot-handler? Hey! a Knitted Icebox for camping and picnics?

By this time next year some of these will have been achieved, and some scorned and abandoned. Some as yet undreamed-of whims will have taken shape. I'm ready for them; my mind is open, my wool-room full of wool, my needles poised, my brain spinning like a Catherine-wheel. There are plenty of pencils—I think—and where did I see that old block of squared paper?

My word, such good fortune. I can only hope the same for you.

APPENDIX OF POSSIBLY UNFAMILIAR TERMS AND IDIOSYNCRATIC PROCEDURES IN THE FOREGOING TEXT.

141

SSK (*slip, slip, knit*)

An excellent decrease of 1 stitch which slants to the left. A substitute for sl 1, K 1, psso: "SSK: slip the first and second stitches *knitwise* one at a time, then insert the tip of left-hand needle into the *fronts* of these two stitches from the left, and knit them together from this position". (From "A Treasury of Knitting Patterns" by Barbara Walker.)

M 1 (*make 1*)

A quick, neat, and fairly invisible way to increase: Put a firm backward loop over the right-hand needle. (A) For absolute symmetry in a double-increase, make the two loops in opposing directions. (A and B)

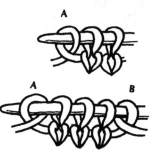

Emily Ocker's Circular Beginning

This is a series of single crochet stitches worked on a loop—as-many-as-you-want stitches; the loop is later tightened. Make a simple loop with the short end below. *With crochet-hook make 2nd loop through this loop (A). With crochet-hook make 3rd loop through 2nd loop (B). Rep from * until there are enough loops on the crochet-hook. Place them on 3 or 4 needles, and continue around. After several inches, pull short end tight, and finish off.

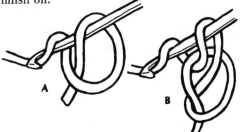

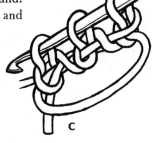

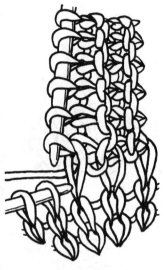

Sideways Border

A firm elastic edge which avoids casting-off. When final row or round of work is finished, *cast on* 6 sts, (or desired number). *K 5, K 2 tog (the last of the 6 sts + 1 st from final row of work). Turn. K 6 Rep from * along (or around) entire border. Weave or sew end to beginning.

Weaving

Having made two swatches as described on p. 47, thread blunt needle with wool and go down through first st at right-hand end of lower piece and up through second stitch. Rep. on upper piece. Go down through second st on lower piece and up through third. Rep on upper piece. And so on.

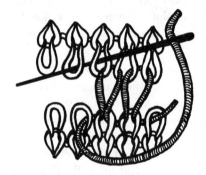

Garter Stitch Weaving

See to it that both threads hang at righthand end of work. Break one and weave with the other. The stitches must lie as in illustration. *Go *down* through first st on lower piece and *up* through second. Go *up* through first st on upper piece and *down* through second. Rep from * on second and third stitches. And so on.

Casting-on Casting-off

An outline-stitch casting-off which deceives. Break the wool, and thread it through a good blunt needle. Hold work with right side towards you, with wool coming from left end. Work from Left to Right: *Keeping working wool above, go into second st from front and first st from back. Pull wool through both sts. Slip first st off. Rep from * This is easiest if sts are taken off the needle.

Sewn Casting-off

Especially good for garter-stitch. Break wool and thread through good blunt needle. Work from Right to Left. *Put needle through first 2 sts from R to L, and pull through (A). Put needle back through first st from L to right, pull through and slip st off (B). Rep from *.

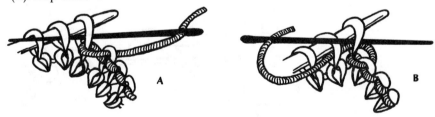

NB

Both these castings-off are supremely useful for the lower edges of a sweater knitted from the top down.

Invisible Casting on

This may be taken out for work to be continued downward. Loosely knot end of wool to a piece of smooth thick twine. Place needle in right hand, holding knot between thumb and forefinger. Hold both threads taut in left hand with twine above. *With needle in right hand come down in *front* of twine, behind and under wool, and up. (A) Now come down *behind* twine, behind and under wool, and up (B). Rep from * until the desired number of sts has been formed by loops of wool around needle and twine, simply ducking down alternately in front of and behind twine and fishing up a loop of wool each time. For first row, knit into all loops as if they were stitches. When time comes to knit down, or weave, from this casting-on, undo loose knot, pull out twine, place revealed stitches on needle and go to it.

A

B

Thumb–Trick

For a 15-stitch thumb.

When you come to the base of the thumb, take a piece of contrasting wool and knit 7 stitches (1 st less than $\frac{1}{2}$ of 15). Put the 7 sts back on left needle and continue as if nothing had happened. When mitten is finished, pull out the piece of wool and 13 sts will appear. Pick them up on 3 needles plus an extra stitch at each end, which should be twisted to avoid a hole. Work to thumb-length, thread wool through all sts and pull tight. Finish off. I like to have the starting-end at the palm-side of the thumb, so that this corner can be finished off extra strongly.

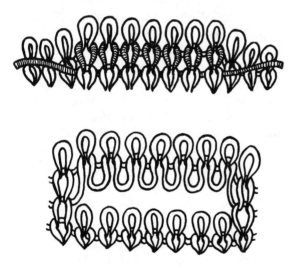

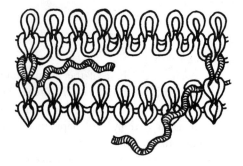

Afterthought Pocket

Decide where you want a pocket and where the middle of the opening will be. Snip one stitch at this point and unravel in either direction. When hole is wide enough, pick up sts and work to desired length on 4 needles. Weave or sew front to back. Pop into place. Neaten corners with unravelled ends.

Need I say that you can also make afterthought thumbs and perform pocket-tricks?

Idiot-Cord

For strings, cords, ties, and borders.

You *must* use two double-pointed needles. Cast on 3 sts. *K 3. *Do not turn.* Slide the sts to the other end of the needle, pull wool firmly, and rep from * to desired length.

Idiot-Cord Border

Gives body and firmness to garter-stitch edges.
*Knit to within 3 sts of end of row. Wool forward, sl 3 as if to purl. Turn. K 1 row. Rep from *. Do not pull wool tightly when turning or border may "hold in" too much.

Short Rows

Frequently used in shaping, for instance, across the back of a sweater.

Work across the back to within 3 or 4 sts of left-hand sideseam. Wool forward, sl 1 st as if to purl, wool back, replace slipped st on lefthand needle. Turn. Purl across to within 3 or 4 sts of righthand sideseam. Wool back, sl 1 st as if to purl, wool forward, replace slipped st on lefthand needle. Turn, and continue working. When you come to the turns, work the tight stitch together with the wool which goes around it. If you do this correctly, you will have a tough time finding out where you turned without holding your knitting up to the light.

Phoney Seams.

To add vertical demarkation lines, and give styling to sweaters and jackets.

Before you cast off, find exact seam-stitch and drop it clear down to the first round. With crochet-hook, * hook the next two threads through it together. Then hook the next thread through *them*. Rep from *, first two threads, then one, until all threads have been hooked up again.

There will be $\frac{2}{3}$ as many rows in the "seam" as there are in the sweater itself.

Index

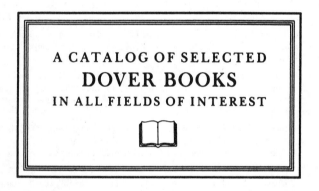

A CATALOG OF SELECTED
DOVER BOOKS
IN ALL FIELDS OF INTEREST

A CATALOG OF SELECTED DOVER
BOOKS IN ALL FIELDS OF INTEREST

CONCERNING THE SPIRITUAL IN ART, Wassily Kandinsky. Pioneering work by father of abstract art. Thoughts on color theory, nature of art. Analysis of earlier masters. 12 illustrations. 80pp. of text. 5⅜ x 8½. 0-486-23411-8

CELTIC ART: The Methods of Construction, George Bain. Simple geometric techniques for making Celtic interlacements, spirals, Kells-type initials, animals, humans, etc. Over 500 illustrations. 160pp. 9 x 12. (Available in U.S. only.) 0-486-22923-8

AN ATLAS OF ANATOMY FOR ARTISTS, Fritz Schider. Most thorough reference work on art anatomy in the world. Hundreds of illustrations, including selections from works by Vesalius, Leonardo, Goya, Ingres, Michelangelo, others. 593 illustrations. 192pp. 7⅛ x 10¼. 0-486-20241-0

CELTIC HAND STROKE-BY-STROKE (Irish Half-Uncial from "The Book of Kells"): An Arthur Baker Calligraphy Manual, Arthur Baker. Complete guide to creating each letter of the alphabet in distinctive Celtic manner. Covers hand position, strokes, pens, inks, paper, more. Illustrated. 48pp. 8¼ x 11. 0-486-24336-2

EASY ORIGAMI, John Montroll. Charming collection of 32 projects (hat, cup, pelican, piano, swan, many more) specially designed for the novice origami hobbyist. Clearly illustrated easy-to-follow instructions insure that even beginning papercrafters will achieve successful results. 48pp. 8¼ x 11. 0-486-27298-2

BLOOMINGDALE'S ILLUSTRATED 1886 CATALOG: Fashions, Dry Goods and Housewares, Bloomingdale Brothers. Famed merchants' extremely rare catalog depicting about 1,700 products: clothing, housewares, firearms, dry goods, jewelry, more. Invaluable for dating, identifying vintage items. Also, copyright-free graphics for artists, designers. Co-published with Henry Ford Museum & Greenfield Village. 160pp. 8¼ x 11. 0-486-25780-0

THE ART OF WORLDLY WISDOM, Baltasar Gracian. "Think with the few and speak with the many," "Friends are a second existence," and "Be able to forget" are among this 1637 volume's 300 pithy maxims. A perfect source of mental and spiritual refreshment, it can be opened at random and appreciated either in brief or at length. 128pp. 5⅜ x 8½. 0-486-44034-6

JOHNSON'S DICTIONARY: A Modern Selection, Samuel Johnson (E. L. McAdam and George Milne, eds.). This modern version reduces the original 1755 edition's 2,300 pages of definitions and literary examples to a more manageable length, retaining the verbal pleasure and historical curiosity of the original. 480pp. 5³⁄₁₆ x 8¼. 0-486-44089-3

ADVENTURES OF HUCKLEBERRY FINN, Mark Twain, Illustrated by E. W. Kemble. A work of eternal richness and complexity, a source of ongoing critical debate, and a literary landmark, Twain's 1885 masterpiece about a barefoot boy's journey of self-discovery has enthralled readers around the world. This handsome clothbound reproduction of the first edition features all 174 of the original black-and-white illustrations. 368pp. 5⅜ x 8½. 0-486-44322-1

STICKLEY CRAFTSMAN FURNITURE CATALOGS, Gustav Stickley and L. & J. G. Stickley. Beautiful, functional furniture in two authentic catalogs from 1910. 594 illustrations, including 277 photos, show settles, rockers, armchairs, reclining chairs, bookcases, desks, tables. 183pp. 6½ x 9¼. 0-486-23838-5

AMERICAN LOCOMOTIVES IN HISTORIC PHOTOGRAPHS: 1858 to 1949, Ron Ziel (ed.). A rare collection of 126 meticulously detailed official photographs, called "builder portraits," of American locomotives that majestically chronicle the rise of steam locomotive power in America. Introduction. Detailed captions. xi+ 129pp. 9 x 12. 0-486-27393-8

AMERICA'S LIGHTHOUSES: An Illustrated History, Francis Ross Holland, Jr. Delightfully written, profusely illustrated fact-filled survey of over 200 American lighthouses since 1716. History, anecdotes, technological advances, more. 240pp. 8 x 10¾. 0-486-25576-X

TOWARDS A NEW ARCHITECTURE, Le Corbusier. Pioneering manifesto by founder of "International School." Technical and aesthetic theories, views of industry, economics, relation of form to function, "mass-production split" and much more. Profusely illustrated. 320pp. 6⅛ x 9¼. (Available in U.S. only.) 0-486-25023-7

HOW THE OTHER HALF LIVES, Jacob Riis. Famous journalistic record, exposing poverty and degradation of New York slums around 1900, by major social reformer. 100 striking and influential photographs. 233pp. 10 x 7⅞. 0-486-22012-5

FRUIT KEY AND TWIG KEY TO TREES AND SHRUBS, William M. Harlow. One of the handiest and most widely used identification aids. Fruit key covers 120 deciduous and evergreen species; twig key 160 deciduous species. Easily used. Over 300 photographs. 126pp. 5⅜ x 8½. 0-486-20511-8

COMMON BIRD SONGS, Dr. Donald J. Borror. Songs of 60 most common U.S. birds: robins, sparrows, cardinals, bluejays, finches, more—arranged in order of increasing complexity. Up to 9 variations of songs of each species.
Cassette and manual 0-486-99911-4

ORCHIDS AS HOUSE PLANTS, Rebecca Tyson Northen. Grow cattleyas and many other kinds of orchids—in a window, in a case, or under artificial light. 63 illustrations. 148pp. 5⅜ x 8½. 0-486-23261-1

MONSTER MAZES, Dave Phillips. Masterful mazes at four levels of difficulty. Avoid deadly perils and evil creatures to find magical treasures. Solutions for all 32 exciting illustrated puzzles. 48pp. 8¼ x 11. 0-486-26005-4

MOZART'S DON GIOVANNI (DOVER OPERA LIBRETTO SERIES), Wolfgang Amadeus Mozart. Introduced and translated by Ellen H. Bleiler. Standard Italian libretto, with complete English translation. Convenient and thoroughly portable—an ideal companion for reading along with a recording or the performance itself. Introduction. List of characters. Plot summary. 121pp. 5¼ x 8½. 0-486-24944-1

FRANK LLOYD WRIGHT'S DANA HOUSE, Donald Hoffmann. Pictorial essay of residential masterpiece with over 160 interior and exterior photos, plans, elevations, sketches and studies. 128pp. 9¼ x 10¾. 0-486-29120-0

THE CLARINET AND CLARINET PLAYING, David Pino. Lively, comprehensive work features suggestions about technique, musicianship, and musical interpretation, as well as guidelines for teaching, making your own reeds, and preparing for public performance. Includes an intriguing look at clarinet history. "A godsend," *The Clarinet,* Journal of the International Clarinet Society. Appendixes. 7 illus. 320pp. 5⅜ x 8½. 0-486-40270-3

HOLLYWOOD GLAMOR PORTRAITS, John Kobal (ed.). 145 photos from 1926-49. Harlow, Gable, Bogart, Bacall; 94 stars in all. Full background on photographers, technical aspects. 160pp. 8⅜ x 11¼. 0-486-23352-9

THE RAVEN AND OTHER FAVORITE POEMS, Edgar Allan Poe. Over 40 of the author's most memorable poems: "The Bells," "Ulalume," "Israfel," "To Helen," "The Conqueror Worm," "Eldorado," "Annabel Lee," many more. Alphabetic lists of titles and first lines. 64pp. 5³⁄₁₆ x 8¼. 0-486-26685-0

PERSONAL MEMOIRS OF U. S. GRANT, Ulysses Simpson Grant. Intelligent, deeply moving firsthand account of Civil War campaigns, considered by many the finest military memoirs ever written. Includes letters, historic photographs, maps and more. 528pp. 6⅛ x 9¼. 0-486-28587-1

POE ILLUSTRATED: Art by Doré, Dulac, Rackham and Others, selected and edited by Jeff A. Menges. More than 100 compelling illustrations, in brilliant color and crisp black-and-white, include scenes from "The Raven," "The Pit and the Pendulum," "The Gold-Bug," and other stories and poems. 96pp. 8⅜ x 11.
0-486-45746-X

RUSSIAN STORIES/RUSSKIE RASSKAZY: A Dual-Language Book, edited by Gleb Struve. Twelve tales by such masters as Chekhov, Tolstoy, Dostoevsky, Pushkin, others. Excellent word-for-word English translations on facing pages, plus teaching and study aids, Russian/English vocabulary, biographical/critical introductions, more. 416pp. 5⅜ x 8½. 0-486-26244-8

PHILADELPHIA THEN AND NOW: 60 Sites Photographed in the Past and Present, Kenneth Finkel and Susan Oyama. Rare photographs of City Hall, Logan Square, Independence Hall, Betsy Ross House, other landmarks juxtaposed with contemporary views. Captures changing face of historic city. Introduction. Captions. 128pp. 8¼ x 11. 0-486-25790-8

NORTH AMERICAN INDIAN LIFE: Customs and Traditions of 23 Tribes, Elsie Clews Parsons (ed.). 27 fictionalized essays by noted anthropologists examine religion, customs, government, additional facets of life among the Winnebago, Crow, Zuni, Eskimo, other tribes. 480pp. 6⅛ x 9¼. 0-486-27377-6

TECHNICAL MANUAL AND DICTIONARY OF CLASSICAL BALLET, Gail Grant. Defines, explains, comments on steps, movements, poses and concepts. 15-page pictorial section. Basic book for student, viewer. 127pp. 5⅜ x 8½.
0-486-21843-0

THE MALE AND FEMALE FIGURE IN MOTION: 60 Classic Photographic Sequences, Eadweard Muybridge. 60 true-action photographs of men and women walking, running, climbing, bending, turning, etc., reproduced from a rare 19th-century masterpiece. vi + 121pp. 9 x 12. 0-486-24745-7

ANIMALS: 1,419 Copyright-Free Illustrations of Mammals, Birds, Fish, Insects, etc., Jim Harter (ed.). Clear wood engravings present, in extremely lifelike poses, over 1,000 species of animals. One of the most extensive pictorial sourcebooks of its kind. Captions. Index. 284pp. 9 x 12. 0-486-23766-4

1001 QUESTIONS ANSWERED ABOUT THE SEASHORE, N. J. Berrill and Jacquelyn Berrill. Queries answered about dolphins, sea snails, sponges, starfish, fishes, shore birds, many others. Covers appearance, breeding, growth, feeding, much more. 305pp. 5¼ x 8¼. 0-486-23366-9

ATTRACTING BIRDS TO YOUR YARD, William J. Weber. Easy-to-follow guide offers advice on how to attract the greatest diversity of birds: birdhouses, feeders, water and waterers, much more. 96pp. 5³⁄₁₆ x 8¼. 0-486-28927-3

MEDICINAL AND OTHER USES OF NORTH AMERICAN PLANTS: A Historical Survey with Special Reference to the Eastern Indian Tribes, Charlotte Erichsen-Brown. Chronological historical citations document 500 years of usage of plants, trees, shrubs native to eastern Canada, northeastern U.S. Also complete identifying information. 343 illustrations. 544pp. 6½ x 9¼. 0-486-25951-X

STORYBOOK MAZES, Dave Phillips. 23 stories and mazes on two-page spreads: Wizard of Oz, Treasure Island, Robin Hood, etc. Solutions. 64pp. 8¼ x 11.
0-486-23628-5

AMERICAN NEGRO SONGS: 230 Folk Songs and Spirituals, Religious and Secular, John W. Work. This authoritative study traces the African influences of songs sung and played by black Americans at work, in church, and as entertainment. The author discusses the lyric significance of such songs as "Swing Low, Sweet Chariot," "John Henry," and others and offers the words and music for 230 songs. Bibliography. Index of Song Titles. 272pp. 6½ x 9¼. 0-486-40271-1

MOVIE-STAR PORTRAITS OF THE FORTIES, John Kobal (ed.). 163 glamor, studio photos of 106 stars of the 1940s: Rita Hayworth, Ava Gardner, Marlon Brando, Clark Gable, many more. 176pp. 8⅜ x 11¼. 0-486-23546-7

YEKL and THE IMPORTED BRIDEGROOM AND OTHER STORIES OF YIDDISH NEW YORK, Abraham Cahan. Film Hester Street based on *Yekl* (1896). Novel, other stories among first about Jewish immigrants on N.Y.'s East Side. 240pp. 5⅜ x 8½. 0-486-22427-9

SELECTED POEMS, Walt Whitman. Generous sampling from *Leaves of Grass*. Twenty-four poems include "I Hear America Singing," "Song of the Open Road," "I Sing the Body Electric," "When Lilacs Last in the Dooryard Bloom'd," "O Captain! My Captain!"–all reprinted from an authoritative edition. Lists of titles and first lines. 128pp. 5³⁄₁₆ x 8¼. 0-486-26878-0

SONGS OF EXPERIENCE: Facsimile Reproduction with 26 Plates in Full Color, William Blake. 26 full-color plates from a rare 1826 edition. Includes "The Tyger," "London," "Holy Thursday," and other poems. Printed text of poems. 48pp. 5¼ x 7.
0-486-24636-1

THE BEST TALES OF HOFFMANN, E. T. A. Hoffmann. 10 of Hoffmann's most important stories: "Nutcracker and the King of Mice," "The Golden Flowerpot," etc. 458pp. 5⅜ x 8½. 0-486-21793-0

THE BOOK OF TEA, Kakuzo Okakura. Minor classic of the Orient: entertaining, charming explanation, interpretation of traditional Japanese culture in terms of tea ceremony. 94pp. 5⅜ x 8½. 0-486-20070-1

FRENCH STORIES/CONTES FRANÇAIS: A Dual-Language Book, Wallace Fowlie. Ten stories by French masters, Voltaire to Camus: "Micromegas" by Voltaire; "The Atheist's Mass" by Balzac; "Minuet" by de Maupassant; "The Guest" by Camus, six more. Excellent English translations on facing pages. Also French-English vocabulary list, exercises, more. 352pp. 5⅜ x 8½. 0-486-26443-2

CHICAGO AT THE TURN OF THE CENTURY IN PHOTOGRAPHS: 122 Historic Views from the Collections of the Chicago Historical Society, Larry A. Viskochil. Rare large-format prints offer detailed views of City Hall, State Street, the Loop, Hull House, Union Station, many other landmarks, circa 1904-1913. Introduction. Captions. Maps. 144pp. 9⅜ x 12¼. 0-486-24656-6

OLD BROOKLYN IN EARLY PHOTOGRAPHS, 1865–1929, William Lee Younger. Luna Park, Gravesend race track, construction of Grand Army Plaza, moving of Hotel Brighton, etc. 157 previously unpublished photographs. 165pp. 8⅞ x 11¾. 0-486-23587-4

THE MYTHS OF THE NORTH AMERICAN INDIANS, Lewis Spence. Rich anthology of the myths and legends of the Algonquins, Iroquois, Pawnees and Sioux, prefaced by an extensive historical and ethnological commentary. 36 illustrations. 480pp. 5⅜ x 8½. 0-486-25967-6

AN ENCYCLOPEDIA OF BATTLES: Accounts of Over 1,560 Battles from 1479 B.C. to the Present, David Eggenberger. Essential details of every major battle in recorded history from the first battle of Megiddo in 1479 B.C. to Grenada in 1984. List of Battle Maps. New Appendix covering the years 1967–1984. Index. 99 illustrations. 544pp. 6½ x 9¼. 0-486-24913-1

SAILING ALONE AROUND THE WORLD, Captain Joshua Slocum. First man to sail around the world, alone, in small boat. One of the great feats of seamanship told in delightful manner. 67 illustrations. 294pp. 5⅜ x 8½. 0-486-20326-3

ANARCHISM AND OTHER ESSAYS, Emma Goldman. Powerful, penetrating, prophetic essays on direct action, role of minorities, prison reform, puritan hypocrisy, violence, etc. 271pp. 5⅜ x 8½. 0-486-22484-8

MYTHS OF THE HINDUS AND BUDDHISTS, Ananda K. Coomaraswamy and Sister Nivedita. Great stories of the epics; deeds of Krishna, Shiva, taken from puranas, Vedas, folk tales; etc. 32 illustrations. 400pp. 5⅜ x 8½. 0-486-21759-0

MY BONDAGE AND MY FREEDOM, Frederick Douglass. Born a slave, Douglass became outspoken force in antislavery movement. The best of Douglass' autobiographies. Graphic description of slave life. 464pp. 5⅜ x 8½. 0-486-22457-0

FOLLOWING THE EQUATOR: A Journey Around the World, Mark Twain. Fascinating humorous account of 1897 voyage to Hawaii, Australia, India, New Zealand, etc. Ironic, bemused reports on peoples, customs, climate, flora and fauna, politics, much more. 197 illustrations. 720pp. 5⅜ x 8½. 0-486-26113-1

GREAT SPEECHES BY AMERICAN WOMEN, edited by James Daley. Here are 21 legendary speeches from the country's most inspirational female voices, including Sojourner Truth, Susan B. Anthony, Eleanor Roosevelt, Hillary Rodham Clinton, Nancy Pelosi, and many others. 192pp. 5³⁄₁₆ x 8¼. 0-486-46141-6

THE MYTHS OF GREECE AND ROME, H. A. Guerber. A classic of mythology, generously illustrated, long prized for its simple, graphic, accurate retelling of the principal myths of Greece and Rome, and for its commentary on their origins and significance. With 64 illustrations by Michelangelo, Raphael, Titian, Rubens, Canova, Bernini and others. 480pp. 5⅜ x 8½. 0-486-27584-1

PSYCHOLOGY OF MUSIC, Carl E. Seashore. Classic work discusses music as a medium from psychological viewpoint. Clear treatment of physical acoustics, auditory apparatus, sound perception, development of musical skills, nature of musical feeling, host of other topics. 88 figures. 408pp. 5⅜ x 8½. 0-486-21851-1

LIFE IN ANCIENT EGYPT, Adolf Erman. Fullest, most thorough, detailed older account with much not in more recent books, domestic life, religion, magic, medicine, commerce, much more. Many illustrations reproduce tomb paintings, carvings, hieroglyphs, etc. 597pp. 5⅜ x 8½. 0-486-22632-8

SUNDIALS, Their Theory and Construction, Albert Waugh. Far and away the best, most thorough coverage of ideas, mathematics concerned, types, construction, adjusting anywhere. Simple, nontechnical treatment allows even children to build several of these dials. Over 100 illustrations. 230pp. 5⅜ x 8½. 0-486-22947-5

GREAT SPEECHES BY AFRICAN AMERICANS: Frederick Douglass, Sojourner Truth, Dr. Martin Luther King, Jr., Barack Obama, and Others, edited by James Daley. Tracing the struggle for freedom and civil rights across two centuries, this anthology comprises speeches by Martin Luther King, Jr., Marcus Garvey, Malcolm X, Barack Obama, and many other influential figures. 160pp. 5³⁄₁₆ x 8¼.
0-486-44761-8

OLD-TIME VIGNETTES IN FULL COLOR, Carol Belanger Grafton (ed.). Over 390 charming, often sentimental illustrations, selected from archives of Victorian graphics—pretty women posing, children playing, food, flowers, kittens and puppies, smiling cherubs, birds and butterflies, much more. All copyright-free. 48pp. 9¼ x 12¼.
0-486-27269-9

PERSPECTIVE FOR ARTISTS, Rex Vicat Cole. Depth, perspective of sky and sea, shadows, much more, not usually covered. 391 diagrams, 81 reproductions of drawings and paintings. 279pp. 5⅜ x 8½. 0-486-22487-2

DRAWING THE LIVING FIGURE, Joseph Sheppard. Innovative approach to artistic anatomy focuses on specifics of surface anatomy, rather than muscles and bones. Over 170 drawings of live models in front, back and side views, and in widely varying poses. Accompanying diagrams. 177 illustrations. Introduction. Index. 144pp. 8⅜ x11¼. 0-486-26723-7

GOTHIC AND OLD ENGLISH ALPHABETS: 100 Complete Fonts, Dan X. Solo. Add power, elegance to posters, signs, other graphics with 100 stunning copyright-free alphabets: Blackstone, Dolbey, Germania, 97 more—including many lower-case, numerals, punctuation marks. 104pp. 8⅛ x 11. 0-486-24695-7

THE BOOK OF WOOD CARVING, Charles Marshall Sayers. Finest book for beginners discusses fundamentals and offers 34 designs. "Absolutely first rate . . . well thought out and well executed."—E. J. Tangerman. 118pp. 7¾ x 10⅝. 0-486-23654-4

ILLUSTRATED CATALOG OF CIVIL WAR MILITARY GOODS: Union Army Weapons, Insignia, Uniform Accessories, and Other Equipment, Schuyler, Hartley, and Graham. Rare, profusely illustrated 1846 catalog includes Union Army uniform and dress regulations, arms and ammunition, coats, insignia, flags, swords, rifles, etc. 226 illustrations. 160pp. 9 x 12. 0-486-24939-5

WOMEN'S FASHIONS OF THE EARLY 1900s: An Unabridged Republication of "New York Fashions, 1909," National Cloak & Suit Co. Rare catalog of mail-order fashions documents women's and children's clothing styles shortly after the turn of the century. Captions offer full descriptions, prices. Invaluable resource for fashion, costume historians. Approximately 725 illustrations. 128pp. 8⅜ x 11¼. 0-486-27276-1

HOW TO DO BEADWORK, Mary White. Fundamental book on craft from simple projects to five-bead chains and woven works. 106 illustrations. 142pp. 5⅜ x 8.
0-486-20697-1

THE 1912 AND 1915 GUSTAV STICKLEY FURNITURE CATALOGS, Gustav Stickley. With over 200 detailed illustrations and descriptions, these two catalogs are essential reading and reference materials and identification guides for Stickley furniture. Captions cite materials, dimensions and prices. 112pp. 6½ x 9¼. 0-486-26676-1

SIX GREAT DIALOGUES: Apology, Crito, Phaedo, Phaedrus, Symposium, The Republic, Plato, translated by Benjamin Jowett. Plato's Dialogues rank among Western civilization's most important and influential philosophical works. These 6 selections of his major works explore a broad range of enduringly relevant issues. Authoritative Jowett translations. 480pp. 5³⁄₁₆ x 8¼. 0-486-45465-7

DEMONOLATRY: An Account of the Historical Practice of Witchcraft, Nicolas Remy, edited with an Introduction and Notes by Montague Summers, translated by E. A. Ashwin. This extremely influential 1595 study was frequently cited at witchcraft trials. In addition to lurid details of satanic pacts and sexual perversity, it presents the particulars of numerous court cases. 240pp. 6½ x 9¼. 0-486-46137-8

VICTORIAN FASHIONS AND COSTUMES FROM HARPER'S BAZAAR, 1867–1898, Stella Blum (ed.). Day costumes, evening wear, sports clothes, shoes, hats, other accessories in over 1,000 detailed engravings. 320pp. 9⅜ x 12¼.
0-486-22990-4

THE LONG ISLAND RAIL ROAD IN EARLY PHOTOGRAPHS, Ron Ziel. Over 220 rare photos, informative text document origin (1844) and development of rail service on Long Island. Vintage views of early trains, locomotives, stations, passengers, crews, much more. Captions. 8⅞ x 11¾. 0-486-26301-0

VOYAGE OF THE LIBERDADE, Joshua Slocum. Great 19th-century mariner's thrilling, first-hand account of the wreck of his ship off South America, the 35-foot boat he built from the wreckage, and its remarkable voyage home. 128pp. 5⅜ x 8½.
0-486-40022-0

TEN BOOKS ON ARCHITECTURE, Vitruvius. The most important book ever written on architecture. Early Roman aesthetics, technology, classical orders, site selection, all other aspects. Morgan translation. 331pp. 5⅜ x 8½. 0-486-20645-9

THE HUMAN FIGURE IN MOTION, Eadweard Muybridge. More than 4,500 stopped-action photos, in action series, showing undraped men, women, children jumping, lying down, throwing, sitting, wrestling, carrying, etc. 390pp. 7⅞ x 10⅝.
0-486-20204-6 Clothbd.

TREES OF THE EASTERN AND CENTRAL UNITED STATES AND CANADA, William M. Harlow. Best one-volume guide to 140 trees. Full descriptions, woodlore, range, etc. Over 600 illustrations. Handy size. 288pp. 4½ x 6⅜. 0-486-20395-6

MY FIRST BOOK OF TCHAIKOVSKY: Favorite Pieces in Easy Piano Arrangements, edited by David Dutkanicz. These special arrangements of favorite Tchaikovsky themes are ideal for beginner pianists, child or adult. Contents include themes from "The Nutcracker," "March Slav," Symphonies Nos. 5 and 6, "Swan Lake," "Sleeping Beauty," and more. 48pp. 8¼ x 11. 0-486-46416-4

BIG BOOK OF MAZES AND LABYRINTHS, Walter Shepherd. 50 mazes and labyrinths in all–classical, solid, ripple, and more–in one great volume. Perfect inexpensive puzzler for clever youngsters. Full solutions. 112pp. 8⅛ x 11. 0-486-22951-3

PIANO TUNING, J. Cree Fischer. Clearest, best book for beginner, amateur. Simple repairs, raising dropped notes, tuning by easy method of flattened fifths. No previous skills needed. 4 illustrations. 201pp. 5⅜ x 8½. 0-486-23267-0

HINTS TO SINGERS, Lillian Nordica. Selecting the right teacher, developing confidence, overcoming stage fright, and many other important skills receive thoughtful discussion in this indispensible guide, written by a world-famous diva of four decades' experience. 96pp. 5⅜ x 8½. 0-486-40094-8

THE COMPLETE NONSENSE OF EDWARD LEAR, Edward Lear. All nonsense limericks, zany alphabets, Owl and Pussycat, songs, nonsense botany, etc., illustrated by Lear. Total of 320pp. 5⅜ x 8½. (Available in U.S. only.) 0-486-20167-8

VICTORIAN PARLOUR POETRY: An Annotated Anthology, Michael R. Turner. 117 gems by Longfellow, Tennyson, Browning, many lesser-known poets. "The Village Blacksmith," "Curfew Must Not Ring Tonight," "Only a Baby Small," dozens more, often difficult to find elsewhere. Index of poets, titles, first lines. xxiii + 325pp. 5⅝ x 8¼. 0-486-27044-0

DUBLINERS, James Joyce. Fifteen stories offer vivid, tightly focused observations of the lives of Dublin's poorer classes. At least one, "The Dead," is considered a masterpiece. Reprinted complete and unabridged from standard edition. 160pp. 5³⁄₁₆ x 8¼. 0-486-26870-5

THE LITTLE RED SCHOOLHOUSE, Eric Sloane. Harkening back to a time when the three Rs stood for reading, 'riting, and religion, Sloane's sketchbook explores the history of early American schools. Includes marvelous illustrations of one-room New England schoolhouses, desks, and benches. 48pp. 8¼ x 11. 0-486-45604-8

THE BOOK OF THE SACRED MAGIC OF ABRAMELIN THE MAGE, translated by S. MacGregor Mathers. Medieval manuscript of ceremonial magic. Basic document in Aleister Crowley, Golden Dawn groups. 268pp. 5⅜ x 8½. 0-486-23211-5

THE BATTLES THAT CHANGED HISTORY, Fletcher Pratt. Eminent historian profiles 16 crucial conflicts, ancient to modern, that changed the course of civilization. 352pp. 5⅜ x 8½. 0-486-41129-X

NEW RUSSIAN-ENGLISH AND ENGLISH-RUSSIAN DICTIONARY, M. A. O'Brien. This is a remarkably handy Russian dictionary, containing a surprising amount of information, including over 70,000 entries. 366pp. 4½ x 6⅛. 0-486-20208-9

NEW YORK IN THE FORTIES, Andreas Feininger. 162 brilliant photographs by the well-known photographer, formerly with *Life* magazine. Commuters, shoppers, Times Square at night, much else from city at its peak. Captions by John von Hartz. 181pp. 9¼ x 10¾. 0-486-23585-8

INDIAN SIGN LANGUAGE, William Tomkins. Over 525 signs developed by Sioux and other tribes. Written instructions and diagrams. Also 290 pictographs. 111pp. 6⅛ x 9¼. 0-486-22029-X

ANATOMY: A Complete Guide for Artists, Joseph Sheppard. A master of figure drawing shows artists how to render human anatomy convincingly. Over 460 illustrations. 224pp. 8⅜ x 11¼. 0-486-27279-6

MEDIEVAL CALLIGRAPHY: Its History and Technique, Marc Drogin. Spirited history, comprehensive instruction manual covers 13 styles (ca. 4th century through 15th). Excellent photographs; directions for duplicating medieval techniques with modern tools. 224pp. 8⅜ x 11¼. 0-486-26142-5

DRIED FLOWERS: How to Prepare Them, Sarah Whitlock and Martha Rankin. Complete instructions on how to use silica gel, meal and borax, perlite aggregate, sand and borax, glycerine and water to create attractive permanent flower arrangements. 12 illustrations. 32pp. 5⅜ x 8½. 0-486-21802-3

EASY-TO-MAKE BIRD FEEDERS FOR WOODWORKERS, Scott D. Campbell. Detailed, simple-to-use guide for designing, constructing, caring for and using feeders. Text, illustrations for 12 classic and contemporary designs. 96pp. 5⅜ x 8½. 0-486-25847-5

THE COMPLETE BOOK OF BIRDHOUSE CONSTRUCTION FOR WOOD-WORKERS, Scott D. Campbell. Detailed instructions, illustrations, tables. Also data on bird habitat and instinct patterns. Bibliography. 3 tables. 63 illustrations in 15 figures. 48pp. 5¼ x 8½. 0-486-24407-5

SCOTTISH WONDER TALES FROM MYTH AND LEGEND, Donald A. Mackenzie. 16 lively tales tell of giants rumbling down mountainsides, of a magic wand that turns stone pillars into warriors, of gods and goddesses, evil hags, powerful forces and more. 240pp. 5⅜ x 8½. 0-486-29677-6

THE HISTORY OF UNDERCLOTHES, C. Willett Cunnington and Phyllis Cunnington. Fascinating, well-documented survey covering six centuries of English undergarments, enhanced with over 100 illustrations: 12th-century laced-up bodice, footed long drawers (1795), 19th-century bustles, l9th-century corsets for men, Victorian "bust improvers," much more. 272pp. 5⅜ x 8¼. 0-486-27124-2

FIRST FRENCH READER: A Beginner's Dual-Language Book, edited and translated by Stanley Appelbaum. This anthology introduces fifty legendary writers—Voltaire, Balzac, Baudelaire, Proust, more—through passages from The Red and the Black, Les Misérables, Madame Bovary, and other classics. Original French text plus English translation on facing pages. 240pp. 5⅜ x 8½. 0-486-46178-5

WILBUR AND ORVILLE: A Biography of the Wright Brothers, Fred Howard. Definitive, crisply written study tells the full story of the brothers' lives and work. A vividly written biography, unparalleled in scope and color, that also captures the spirit of an extraordinary era. 560pp. 6⅛ x 9¼. 0-486-40297-5

THE ARTS OF THE SAILOR: Knotting, Splicing and Ropework, Hervey Garrett Smith. Indispensable shipboard reference covers tools, basic knots and useful hitches; handsewing and canvas work, more. Over 100 illustrations. Delightful reading for sea lovers. 256pp. 5⅜ x 8½. 0-486-26440-8

FRANK LLOYD WRIGHT'S FALLINGWATER: The House and Its History, Second, Revised Edition, Donald Hoffmann. A total revision—both in text and illustrations—of the standard document on Fallingwater, the boldest, most personal architectural statement of Wright's mature years, updated with valuable new material from the recently opened Frank Lloyd Wright Archives. "Fascinating"—*The New York Times.* 116 illustrations. 128pp. 9¼ x 10¾. 0-486-27430-6

PHOTOGRAPHIC SKETCHBOOK OF THE CIVIL WAR, Alexander Gardner. 100 photos taken on field during the Civil War. Famous shots of Manassas Harper's Ferry, Lincoln, Richmond, slave pens, etc. 244pp. 10⅝ x 8¼. 0-486-22731-6

FIVE ACRES AND INDEPENDENCE, Maurice G. Kains. Great back-to-the-land classic explains basics of self-sufficient farming. The one book to get. 95 illustrations. 397pp. 5⅜ x 8½. 0-486-20974-1

A MODERN HERBAL, Margaret Grieve. Much the fullest, most exact, most useful compilation of herbal material. Gigantic alphabetical encyclopedia, from aconite to zedoary, gives botanical information, medical properties, folklore, economic uses, much else. Indispensable to serious reader. 161 illustrations. 888pp. 6½ x 9¼. 2-vol. set. (Available in U.S. only.)　　　Vol. I: 0-486-22798-7　　　Vol. II: 0-486-22799-5

HIDDEN TREASURE MAZE BOOK, Dave Phillips. Solve 34 challenging mazes accompanied by heroic tales of adventure. Evil dragons, people-eating plants, blood-thirsty giants, many more dangerous adversaries lurk at every twist and turn. 34 mazes, stories, solutions. 48pp. 8¼ x 11.　　　　　　　　　　0-486-24566-7

LETTERS OF W. A. MOZART, Wolfgang A. Mozart. Remarkable letters show bawdy wit, humor, imagination, musical insights, contemporary musical world; includes some letters from Leopold Mozart. 276pp. 5⅜ x 8½.　　　0-486-22859-2

BASIC PRINCIPLES OF CLASSICAL BALLET, Agrippina Vaganova. Great Russian theoretician, teacher explains methods for teaching classical ballet. 118 illustrations. 175pp. 5⅜ x 8½.　　　　　　　　　　　　　0-486-22036-2

THE JUMPING FROG, Mark Twain. Revenge edition. The original story of The Celebrated Jumping Frog of Calaveras County, a hapless French translation, and Twain's hilarious "retranslation" from the French. 12 illustrations. 66pp. 5⅜ x 8½.
0-486-22686-7

BEST REMEMBERED POEMS, Martin Gardner (ed.). The 126 poems in this superb collection of 19th- and 20th-century British and American verse range from Shelley's "To a Skylark" to the impassioned "Renascence" of Edna St. Vincent Millay and to Edward Lear's whimsical "The Owl and the Pussycat." 224pp. 5⅜ x 8½.
0-486-27165-X

COMPLETE SONNETS, William Shakespeare. Over 150 exquisite poems deal with love, friendship, the tyranny of time, beauty's evanescence, death and other themes in language of remarkable power, precision and beauty. Glossary of archaic terms. 80pp. 5³⁄₁₆ x 8¼.　　　　　　　　　　　　　　　　0-486-26686-9

HISTORIC HOMES OF THE AMERICAN PRESIDENTS, Second, Revised Edition, Irvin Haas. A traveler's guide to American Presidential homes, most open to the public, depicting and describing homes occupied by every American President from George Washington to George Bush. With visiting hours, admission charges, travel routes. 175 photographs. Index. 160pp. 8¼ x 11.　　　0-486-26751-2

THE WIT AND HUMOR OF OSCAR WILDE, Alvin Redman (ed.). More than 1,000 ripostes, paradoxes, wisecracks: Work is the curse of the drinking classes; I can resist everything except temptation; etc. 258pp. 5⅜ x 8½.　　　0-486-20602-5

SHAKESPEARE LEXICON AND QUOTATION DICTIONARY, Alexander Schmidt. Full definitions, locations, shades of meaning in every word in plays and poems. More than 50,000 exact quotations. 1,485pp. 6½ x 9¼. 2-vol. set.
Vol. 1: 0-486-22726-X　　　Vol. 2: 0-486-22727-8

SELECTED POEMS, Emily Dickinson. Over 100 best-known, best-loved poems by one of America's foremost poets, reprinted from authoritative early editions. No comparable edition at this price. Index of first lines. 64pp. 5³⁄₁₆ x 8¼. 0-486-26466-1

THE INSIDIOUS DR. FU-MANCHU, Sax Rohmer. The first of the popular mystery series introduces a pair of English detectives to their archnemesis, the diabolical Dr. Fu-Manchu. Flavorful atmosphere, fast-paced action, and colorful characters enliven this classic of the genre. 208pp. 5³⁄₁₆ x 8¼.　　　　0-486-29898-1

THE MALLEUS MALEFICARUM OF KRAMER AND SPRENGER, translated by Montague Summers. Full text of most important witchhunter's "bible," used by both Catholics and Protestants. 278pp. 6⅝ x 10. 0-486-22802-9

SPANISH STORIES/CUENTOS ESPAÑOLES: A Dual-Language Book, Angel Flores (ed.). Unique format offers 13 great stories in Spanish by Cervantes, Borges, others. Faithful English translations on facing pages. 352pp. 5⅜ x 8½.
0-486-25399-6

GARDEN CITY, LONG ISLAND, IN EARLY PHOTOGRAPHS, 1869–1919, Mildred H. Smith. Handsome treasury of 118 vintage pictures, accompanied by carefully researched captions, document the Garden City Hotel fire (1899), the Vanderbilt Cup Race (1908), the first airmail flight departing from the Nassau Boulevard Aerodrome (1911), and much more. 96pp. 8⅞ x 11¾. 0-486-40669-5

OLD QUEENS, N.Y., IN EARLY PHOTOGRAPHS, Vincent F. Seyfried and William Asadorian. Over 160 rare photographs of Maspeth, Jamaica, Jackson Heights, and other areas. Vintage views of DeWitt Clinton mansion, 1939 World's Fair and more. Captions. 192pp. 8⅞ x 11. 0-486-26358-4

CAPTURED BY THE INDIANS: 15 Firsthand Accounts, 1750-1870, Frederick Drimmer. Astounding true historical accounts of grisly torture, bloody conflicts, relentless pursuits, miraculous escapes and more, by people who lived to tell the tale. 384pp. 5⅜ x 8½. 0-486-24901-8

THE WORLD'S GREAT SPEECHES (Fourth Enlarged Edition), Lewis Copeland, Lawrence W. Lamm, and Stephen J. McKenna. Nearly 300 speeches provide public speakers with a wealth of updated quotes and inspiration–from Pericles' funeral oration and William Jennings Bryan's "Cross of Gold Speech" to Malcolm X's powerful words on the Black Revolution and Earl of Spenser's tribute to his sister, Diana, Princess of Wales. 944pp. 5⅜ x 8⅜. 0-486-40903-1

THE BOOK OF THE SWORD, Sir Richard F. Burton. Great Victorian scholar/adventurer's eloquent, erudite history of the "queen of weapons"–from prehistory to early Roman Empire. Evolution and development of early swords, variations (sabre, broadsword, cutlass, scimitar, etc.), much more. 336pp. 6⅛ x 9¼.
0-486-25434-8

AUTOBIOGRAPHY: The Story of My Experiments with Truth, Mohandas K. Gandhi. Boyhood, legal studies, purification, the growth of the Satyagraha (nonviolent protest) movement. Critical, inspiring work of the man responsible for the freedom of India. 480pp. 5⅜ x 8½. (Available in U.S. only.) 0-486-24593-4

CELTIC MYTHS AND LEGENDS, T. W. Rolleston. Masterful retelling of Irish and Welsh stories and tales. Cuchulain, King Arthur, Deirdre, the Grail, many more. First paperback edition. 58 full-page illustrations. 512pp. 5⅜ x 8½. 0-486-26507-2

THE PRINCIPLES OF PSYCHOLOGY, William James. Famous long course complete, unabridged. Stream of thought, time perception, memory, experimental methods; great work decades ahead of its time. 94 figures. 1,391pp. 5⅜ x 8½. 2-vol. set.
Vol. I: 0-486-20381-6   Vol. II: 0-486-20382-4

THE WORLD AS WILL AND REPRESENTATION, Arthur Schopenhauer. Definitive English translation of Schopenhauer's life work, correcting more than 1,000 errors, omissions in earlier translations. Translated by E. F. J. Payne. Total of 1,269pp. 5⅜ x 8½. 2-vol. set.   Vol. 1: 0-486-21761-2   Vol. 2: 0-486-21762-0

CATALOG OF DOVER BOOKS

MAGIC AND MYSTERY IN TIBET, Madame Alexandra David-Neel. Experiences among lamas, magicians, sages, sorcerers, Bonpa wizards. A true psychic discovery. 32 illustrations. 321pp. 5⅜ x 8½. (Available in U.S. only.) 0-486-22682-4

THE EGYPTIAN BOOK OF THE DEAD, E. A. Wallis Budge. Complete reproduction of Ani's papyrus, finest ever found. Full hieroglyphic text, interlinear transliteration, word-for-word translation, smooth translation. 533pp. 6½ x 9¼.

0-486-21866-X

HISTORIC COSTUME IN PICTURES, Braun & Schneider. Over 1,450 costumed figures in clearly detailed engravings–from dawn of civilization to end of 19th century. Captions. Many folk costumes. 256pp. 8⅜ x 11¾. 0-486-23150-X

MATHEMATICS FOR THE NONMATHEMATICIAN, Morris Kline. Detailed, college-level treatment of mathematics in cultural and historical context, with numerous exercises. Recommended Reading Lists. Tables. Numerous figures. 641pp. 5⅜ x 8½. 0-486-24823-2

PROBABILISTIC METHODS IN THE THEORY OF STRUCTURES, Isaac Elishakoff. Well-written introduction covers the elements of the theory of probability from two or more random variables, the reliability of such multivariable structures, the theory of random function, Monte Carlo methods of treating problems incapable of exact solution, and more. Examples. 502pp. 5⅜ x 8½. 0-486-40691-1

THE RIME OF THE ANCIENT MARINER, Gustave Doré, S. T. Coleridge. Doré's finest work; 34 plates capture moods, subtleties of poem. Flawless full-size reproductions printed on facing pages with authoritative text of poem. "Beautiful. Simply beautiful."–*Publisher's Weekly.* 77pp. 9¼ x 12. 0-486-22305-1

SCULPTURE: Principles and Practice, Louis Slobodkin. Step-by-step approach to clay, plaster, metals, stone; classical and modern. 253 drawings, photos. 255pp. 8⅛ x 11. 0-486-22960-2

THE INFLUENCE OF SEA POWER UPON HISTORY, 1660–1783, A. T. Mahan. Influential classic of naval history and tactics still used as text in war colleges. First paperback edition. 4 maps. 24 battle plans. 640pp. 5⅜ x 8½. 0-486-25509-3

THE STORY OF THE TITANIC AS TOLD BY ITS SURVIVORS, Jack Winocour (ed.). What it was really like. Panic, despair, shocking inefficiency, and a little heroism. More thrilling than any fictional account. 26 illustrations. 320pp. 5⅜ x 8½.

0-486-20610-6

ONE TWO THREE . . . INFINITY: Facts and Speculations of Science, George Gamow. Great physicist's fascinating, readable overview of contemporary science: number theory, relativity, fourth dimension, entropy, genes, atomic structure, much more. 128 illustrations. Index. 352pp. 5⅜ x 8½. 0-486-25664-2

DALÍ ON MODERN ART: The Cuckolds of Antiquated Modern Art, Salvador Dalí. Influential painter skewers modern art and its practitioners. Outrageous evaluations of Picasso, Cézanne, Turner, more. 15 renderings of paintings discussed. 44 calligraphic decorations by Dalí. 96pp. 5⅜ x 8½. (Available in U.S. only.) 0-486-29220-7

ANTIQUE PLAYING CARDS: A Pictorial History, Henry René D'Allemagne. Over 900 elaborate, decorative images from rare playing cards (14th–20th centuries): Bacchus, death, dancing dogs, hunting scenes, royal coats of arms, players cheating, much more. 96pp. 9¼ x 12¼. 0-486-29265-7

MAKING FURNITURE MASTERPIECES: 30 Projects with Measured Drawings, Franklin H. Gottshall. Step-by-step instructions, illustrations for constructing handsome, useful pieces, among them a Sheraton desk, Chippendale chair, Spanish desk, Queen Anne table and a William and Mary dressing mirror. 224pp. 8⅛ x 11¼.
0-486-29338-6

NORTH AMERICAN INDIAN DESIGNS FOR ARTISTS AND CRAFTSPEOPLE, Eva Wilson. Over 360 authentic copyright-free designs adapted from Navajo blankets, Hopi pottery, Sioux buffalo hides, more. Geometrics, symbolic figures, plant and animal motifs, etc. 128pp. 8⅜ x 11. (Not for sale in the United Kingdom.) 0-486-25341-4

THE FOSSIL BOOK: A Record of Prehistoric Life, Patricia V. Rich et al. Profusely illustrated definitive guide covers everything from single-celled organisms and dinosaurs to birds and mammals and the interplay between climate and man. Over 1,500 illustrations. 760pp. 7½ x 10⅛. 0-486-29371-8

VICTORIAN ARCHITECTURAL DETAILS: Designs for Over 700 Stairs, Mantels, Doors, Windows, Cornices, Porches, and Other Decorative Elements, A. J. Bicknell & Company. Everything from dormer windows and piazzas to balconies and gable ornaments. Also includes elevations and floor plans for handsome, private residences and commercial structures. 80pp. 9⅜ x 12¼. 0-486-44015-X

WESTERN ISLAMIC ARCHITECTURE: A Concise Introduction, John D. Hoag. Profusely illustrated critical appraisal compares and contrasts Islamic mosques and palaces–from Spain and Egypt to other areas in the Middle East. 139 illustrations. 128pp. 6 x 9. 0-486-43760-4

CHINESE ARCHITECTURE: A Pictorial History, Liang Ssu-ch'eng. More than 240 rare photographs and drawings depict temples, pagodas, tombs, bridges, and imperial palaces comprising much of China's architectural heritage. 152 halftones, 94 diagrams. 232pp. 10¾ x 9⅞. 0-486-43999-2

THE RENAISSANCE: Studies in Art and Poetry, Walter Pater. One of the most talked-about books of the 19th century, *The Renaissance* combines scholarship and philosophy in an innovative work of cultural criticism that examines the achievements of Botticelli, Leonardo, Michelangelo, and other artists. "The holy writ of beauty."–Oscar Wilde. 160pp. 5⅜ x 8½. 0-486-44025-7

A TREATISE ON PAINTING, Leonardo da Vinci. The great Renaissance artist's practical advice on drawing and painting techniques covers anatomy, perspective, composition, light and shadow, and color. A classic of art instruction, it features 48 drawings by Nicholas Poussin and Leon Battista Alberti. 192pp. 5⅜ x 8½.
0-486-44155-5

THE ESSENTIAL JEFFERSON, Thomas Jefferson, edited by John Dewey. This extraordinary primer offers a superb survey of Jeffersonian thought. It features writings on political and economic philosophy, morals and religion, intellectual freedom and progress, education, secession, slavery, and more. 176pp. 5⅜ x 8½.
0-486-46599-3

WASHINGTON IRVING'S RIP VAN WINKLE, Illustrated by Arthur Rackham. Lovely prints that established artist as a leading illustrator of the time and forever etched into the popular imagination a classic of Catskill lore. 51 full-color plates. 80pp. 8⅜ x 11. 0-486-44242-X

HENSCHE ON PAINTING, John W. Robichaux. Basic painting philosophy and methodology of a great teacher, as expounded in his famous classes and workshops on Cape Cod. 7 illustrations in color on covers. 80pp. 5⅜ x 8½. 0-486-43728-0

CATALOG OF DOVER BOOKS

LIGHT AND SHADE: A Classic Approach to Three-Dimensional Drawing, Mrs. Mary P. Merrifield. Handy reference clearly demonstrates principles of light and shade by revealing effects of common daylight, sunshine, and candle or artificial light on geometrical solids. 13 plates. 64pp. 5⅜ x 8½. 0-486-44143-1

ASTROLOGY AND ASTRONOMY: A Pictorial Archive of Signs and Symbols, Ernst and Johanna Lehner. Treasure trove of stories, lore, and myth, accompanied by more than 300 rare illustrations of planets, the Milky Way, signs of the zodiac, comets, meteors, and other astronomical phenomena. 192pp. 8⅜ x 11.

0-486-43981-X

JEWELRY MAKING: Techniques for Metal, Tim McCreight. Easy-to-follow instructions and carefully executed illustrations describe tools and techniques, use of gems and enamels, wire inlay, casting, and other topics. 72 line illustrations and diagrams. 176pp. 8¼ x 10⅞. 0-486-44043-5

MAKING BIRDHOUSES: Easy and Advanced Projects, Gladstone Califf. Easy-to-follow instructions include diagrams for everything from a one-room house for bluebirds to a forty-two-room structure for purple martins. 56 plates; 4 figures. 80pp. 8¾ x 6⅜. 0-486-44183-0

LITTLE BOOK OF LOG CABINS: How to Build and Furnish Them, William S. Wicks. Handy how-to manual, with instructions and illustrations for building cabins in the Adirondack style, fireplaces, stairways, furniture, beamed ceilings, and more. 102 line drawings. 96pp. 8¾ x 6⅜. 0-486-44259-4

THE SEASONS OF AMERICA PAST, Eric Sloane. From "sugaring time" and strawberry picking to Indian summer and fall harvest, a whole year's activities described in charming prose and enhanced with 79 of the author's own illustrations. 160pp. 8¼ x 11. 0-486-44220-9

THE METROPOLIS OF TOMORROW, Hugh Ferriss. Generous, prophetic vision of the metropolis of the future, as perceived in 1929. Powerful illustrations of towering structures, wide avenues, and rooftop parks—all features in many of today's modern cities. 59 illustrations. 144pp. 8¼ x 11. 0-486-43727-2

THE PATH TO ROME, Hilaire Belloc. This 1902 memoir abounds in lively vignettes from a vanished time, recounting a pilgrimage on foot across the Alps and Apennines in order to "see all Europe which the Christian Faith has saved." 77 of the author's original line drawings complement his sparkling prose. 272pp. 5⅜ x 8½.

0-486-44001-X

THE HISTORY OF RASSELAS: Prince of Abissinia, Samuel Johnson. Distinguished English writer attacks eighteenth-century optimism and man's unrealistic estimates of what life has to offer. 112pp. 5⅜ x 8½. 0-486-44094-X

A VOYAGE TO ARCTURUS, David Lindsay. A brilliant flight of pure fancy, where wild creatures crowd the fantastic landscape and demented torturers dominate victims with their bizarre mental powers. 272pp. 5⅜ x 8½. 0-486-44198-9